RESTRUCTURING SOUTH AFRICA

Also by John D. Brewer

AFTER SOWETO
BLACK AND BLUE: Policing in South Africa
*CAN SOUTH AFRICA SURVIVE? (*editor*)
INSIDE THE RUC
MOSLEY'S MEN
POLICE, PUBLIC ORDER AND THE STATE (*with Adrian Guelke,
Ian Hume, Edward Moxon-Browne and Rick Wilford*)
THE ROYAL IRISH CONSTABULARY: An Oral History

From the same publishers

Restructuring South Africa

Edited by

John D. Brewer
Professor of Sociology
The Queen's University of Belfast

St. Martin's Press

First published in Great Britain 1994 by
THE MACMILLAN PRESS LTD
Houndmills, Basingstoke, Hampshire RG21 2XS
and London
Companies and representatives
throughout the world

A catalogue record for this book is available
from the British Library.

ISBN 0–333–60591–8

Printed in Great Britain by
Antony Rowe Ltd
Chippenham, Wiltshire

First published in the United States of America 1994 by
Scholarly and Reference Division,
ST. MARTIN'S PRESS, INC.,
175 Fifth Avenue,
New York, N.Y. 10010

ISBN 0–312–10583–5

Library of Congress Cataloging-in-Publication Data
Restructuring South Africa / edited by John D. Brewer.
p.   cm.
Includes index.
ISBN 0–312–10583–5
1. South Africa—Social conditions—1961–   —Congresses.   2. South
Africa—Politics and government—1978–   —Congresses.   I. Brewer,
John D.
HN800.A8R47   1994
306'.0968—dc20
                                              93–29949
                                                 CIP

Contents

List of Maps (and Table)

Preface

In 1989 Macmillan published a book that I edited, entitled *Can South Africa Survive?: Five Minutes to Midnight*. It was based on an international conference organised by Heribert Weiland and myself in 1987, held at the University of Amsterdam under the auspices of the European Consortium for Political Research. The conference was designed to reassess the controversial thesis of R. W. Johnson, in *How Long Will South Africa Survive?*, published by Macmillan in 1977, just after the outbreak of widespread civil unrest and the onset of renewed international pressure against the country. Johnson predicted that South Africa's apartheid system would survive: the hands of the clock were stuck ominously at five minutes to midnight. Contributors to the edited collection re-examined Johnson's argument in the light of events inside South Africa, politically and economically, as well as in the region and internationally. We concluded that significant developments had occurred and that the hands of the clock were beginning to waver.

How right we were was shown in 1989, the year in which the edited collection was published: Frederick de Klerk, leader of the governing National Party, dismantled all the legal pillars supporting apartheid. Within a few months, he legalised all opposition movements and released political prisoners, Nelson Mandela among them, and set a significant process of reform in progress. For the first time in its history as a nation, South Africa looked as if it was becoming a non-racial democracy, and a just and more equitable society.

However, it is very apparent that the period of transition is proving to be problematic. Accusations of political malevolence and malpractice are rife on all sides, atrocities have risen in scale and frequency, and violence continues. Burying the corpse of apartheid is proving to be protracted and difficult, and may yet well result in the still-birth of the new South Africa.

In 1992 I was invited by John McCracken, President of the African Studies Association of the United Kingdom, to direct a workshop at its annual conference, held in the University of Stirling, to assess the prospects of order and disorder in the new

South Africa. Not unnaturally, contributors to that workshop focused on the problems of transition, and the likely prospects of South Africa becoming a peaceful, just, equitable and democratic society. With the old apartheid system having, thankfully, failed to survive, the issue for participants in 1992 became the birth and survival of the new South Africa.

This is a measure of how far the agenda had changed between the two conferences: in 1992 we were at the other side of midnight, and discussing the likelihood of moving to dawn. *Restructuring South Africa* represents revised versions of papers presented at that workshop, and discusses the prospects of South Africa reaching the new era of justice, democracy, peace and stability. We do not address what the state in the new South Africa should do, but what is possible for it to do in some key areas, such as the constitution, crime, policing, educational desegregation, and the containment of violence.

As editor of the volume, it falls to me to acknowledge the people who have contributed to it. John McCracken and the African Studies Association of the United Kingdom must be thanked for bringing us together to consider these issues. We would like to acknowledge the positive contribution made to each paper by all contributors at the workshop and the audience who attended. Unfortunately, it has not been possible to publish all the papers presented at the workshop, but every paper here has benefited from the fruitful and constructive interchanges that took place during the workshop.

John D. Brewer

Belfast, 1993

Notes on the Contributors

John D. Brewer is Professor of Sociology at The Queen's University of Belfast. In 1989 he was Visiting Fellow at Yale University, and for the summer of 1992 he was Visiting Scholar at St John's College, Oxford. His major publications cover South Africa, Northern Ireland and the police. His books are: *Mosley's Men* (Gower, 1984); *After Soweto* (Oxford University Press, 1986); *Police, Public Order and the State* (Macmillan, 1988; co-authored); *The Royal Irish Constabulary: An Oral History* (Institute of Irish Studies, 1990); *Inside the RUC* (Oxford University Press, 1991); *Black and Blue: Policing in South Africa* (Oxford University Press, 1994). He is also editor of *Can South Africa Survive?* (Macmillan, 1989). He has participated in four international study groups on aspects of South Africa and its future.

Adrian Guelke is Jan Smuts Professor of International Relations at the University of the Witwatersrand. He lectured in the Department of Politics at The Queen's University of Belfast between 1975 and 1992. He is the author of *Northern Ireland: The International Perspective* (Gill and Macmillan, 1988), and a co-author of *Police, Public Order and the State* (Macmillan, 1988).

Anthony Lemon is an Official Fellow and Senior Tutor at Mansfield College and Lecturer in Geography at Oxford University. He is a social and political geographer with long-standing interests in South Africa, where he has held Visiting Lectureships and Research Fellowships at the universities of Natal (Pietermaritzburg), Rhodes, Cape Town, Stellenbosch and Witwatersrand, as well as the University of Zimbabwe. His publications include *Apartheid: A Geography of Separation* (1976), *Apartheid in Transition* (1987), *Homes Apart: South Africa's Segregated Cities* (1991), and articles on the geography of elections, constitutional change, international relations, South Africa's Indian minority, urban apartheid, and educational change.

Johan Olivier is Director of the Centre for Conflict Analysis at the Human Sciences Research Council in South Africa. He holds a Ph.D in sociology from Cornell University in the United States. He is engaged in extensive research into civil unrest and political violence in South Africa, as well as collaborating with colleagues at Stanford University in the United States on a comparative study of racial and ethnic conflict in South Africa and the United States. He is a member of an international panel of experts on mass demonstrations which advised the Goldstone Commission. He is a member of the National Peace Secretariat's sub-committee on research and peace. He was visiting lecturer at the University of Cape Town, and has been teaching as guest lecturer at the University of Pretoria since 1991. He is a member of the South African Sociological Association, the American Sociological Association and the International Sociological Association.

Kierin O'Malley studied law at the University of Stellenbosch and politics at the University of Cape Town. He currently lectures in the Department of Political Science at the University of South Africa.

Mark Shaw has a doctorate from the University of the Witwatersrand and is a Research Officer at the Centre for Policy Studies in Johannesburg. In this capacity, he is currently researching political violence on the Reef and in Natal, with particular reference to the operation of the National Peace Accord at the local level.

Rupert Taylor has a doctorate from the University of Kent, and is Senior Lecturer in Political Studies at the University of the Witwatersrand. His recent publications on South Africa include articles in *Telos*, *Race and Class*, and *Transformations*.

Ronald Weitzer is an Associate Professor of Sociology at George Washington University in Washington DC, and holds a doctorate from the University of California at Berkeley. He has published extensively on policing in divided societies, and is the author of *Transforming Settler Societies: Communal Conflict and Internal Security in Northern Ireland and Zimbabwe* (University of California Press, 1990). He has just completed a book on police–community relations in Northern Ireland, entitled *Policing Under Fire: Ethnic Conflict and Police–Community Relations in Northern Ireland*, to be published by State University of New York Press.

Introduction: South Africa in Transition

John D. Brewer

INTRODUCTION

If for decades in South Africa the hands of the clock were stuck firmly at five minutes to midnight, they have now moved forward and the clock approaches dawn – a society where there is democracy, peace, justice and stability. But while getting to midnight was protracted and problematic enough, moving beyond it is equally fraught. If apartheid is dead, the new South Africa is yet still a weakling. Constitutional talks are floundering, political parties seem bent on self-interest, the paramilitary organisations continue their violence, such that atrocity piles upon atrocity, the white and black right wings threaten, crime levels have soared, and some promised reforms seem slow in their pace, notably constitutional changes, reform of the police and educational desegregation.

Two remarks come to mind when thinking about South Africa's transition to a just, equitable and democratic society, both with their origins in China. On being asked once about his thoughts on the effects of the French Revolution, Chairman Mao is reputed to have said that it was too early to judge. Against this cautious standard, it seems worthless at this early stage to venture opinion on South Africa's restructuring, or the likelihood of South Africa moving much beyond midnight. But Mao's advice is poor because it permits no reflection whatsoever, and an older Chinese proverb is worth noting: a journey of a thousand years starts with one small step. It is our contention that something significant has begun in South Africa and the small steps taken since 1989, on what is hopefully a long journey, are worth addressing, even at this early stage, in order to see what further steps can or should be taken, what care should be exercised in future steps, whether the stride

1

should speed its pace, and whether the distance travelled so far is sufficient for the time taken.

The chapters in this volume are written in the hope that the small steps taken since 1989 are, indeed, the start of South Africa's final long journey toward democracy, peace, justice and stability. But they are also written in the knowledge that hope is not enough to ensure that this sort of society is realised. Thus, they address some of the practical issues and problems that are important in the restructuring of South Africa. Chapters fall into two kinds. Some examine critical problems which define the chaos of the transitional period (political violence, the Natal conflict, crime), in order to evaluate the prospects of the disorder coming to an end. Others address key areas of reform by which peace and stability could be restored (policing, educational de-segregation and the constitution), to identify the issues and problems involved in the reform and what needs to be resolved or achieved in order for peace and stability to be realised. The final chapter discusses the role of external mediation both in achieving and underwriting the transition to a peaceful, democratic and just society.

This is not a comprehensive review of all the issues involved in restructuring South Africa. No consideration is given, for example, to the economy, administrative and civil service re-arrangements, the right wing or the military. By contrast, however, the volume does not focus exclusively on the political dimension. It is a common misconception that successful consti-tutional negotiations will bring peace and stability. Democrat-isation of the polity is important in order to redistribute power through new governing structures, and to establish mechanisms of political accountability and representative forums for debate. A legitimate government can achieve a great deal in South Africa, but the chaos and disorder of the transitional period indicate there to be a huge gap between leaders and their mass constituencies. The political elites currently involved in con-stitutional talks are divorced from large parts of the population whose primary concerns are to obtain employment, decent hous-ing, a good education, and protection from crime and random killings. Political negotiations are marginal to their lives, and part of the requirement in the transitional phase is to ensure that South Africa is restructured sufficiently to address these other problems.

Democratisation of the polity is thus not the only restructuring that needs to take place. Therefore, in addition to an examination of constitutional negotiations, this volume addresses issues such as crime, the ending of violence generally and the Natal conflict particularly, reform of the police and of the education system, as well as considering the likely role of external mediation in underwriting South Africa's restructuring.

The intention in the rest of this introductory chapter is to explore some of the problems of transition which make it vitally necessary that the task of reconstruction be finished early and accomplished successfully. The problems evident in the transitional phase include those posed by the right-wing threat, political violence, emanating from both right and left, crime and disorder, the economic costs of reconstruction, the need for reform to speed its pace, disagreements over political negotiations, the need to depoliticise ethnicity, and the problems caused by the natural fears and insecurities about the future among whites and the raised expectations for socio-economic redistribution among blacks.

FROM RHETORIC TO RECONSTRUCTION

The transition from apartheid to the new South Africa is in essence a transition from rhetoric to reconstruction – from talk about reform to achieving the necessary restructuring of institutions, relationships and processes. Apartheid infected people's attitudes as well, but attitudes are less amenable to reconstruction than institutions. Nonetheless, the psyche of apartheid still permeates the thinking of many people in South Africa and this is one of the most critical problems of the transition. It infects the white right wing, as well as the conservative black groups in the former homelands. Fears and insecurities about the future, whether about crime, job security or political stability, affect moderates as well. Giliomee and Schlemmer (1989: p. v) once wrote that most whites desired the abolition of apartheid, provided it could occur without major upheaval. It was impossible to think that such a social formation could change without upheaval. The revenge murders of whites, the shooting dead of unarmed protesters by police, the orgy of looting and crime by gangs, and the appearance of squatter camps for homeless white beggars, give moderate South Africans a frightening glimpse of what the future might hold. But structural reconstruction can reduce crime, achieve economic growth and create legitimate and democratic political institutions in order to lessen the fears and insecurities of most South Africans. It is the opposition to any reconstruction among the right wing, based on irrational fears and insecurities, that threatens the transition more than the fears of the moderates.

The right wing threatens mainly through its recourse to violence, which is used both to destabilise an already tense situation by means of political assassination (such as that of Chris Hani) and random killings and atrocities, and also to prevent reformers, black or white, from winning free elections. Some of the atrocities have been truly appalling, such as attacks on busloads of innocent schoolchildren, the only purpose of which is to incite a conflagration. Jan Smith, leader of the far-right Church of the Creator, which espouses unreconstructed apartheid, said in the *The Sunday Times* (London) in April 1993:

> What we need rapidly now is further confrontation and polarisation between the races. Something like the killing of Nelson Mandela, that will drive the blacks out of control and force the security forces to use massive forces against them.

In May 1993 a conspiracy was uncovered to assassinate Joe Slovo, leader of the South African Communist Party, which, if it had been successful, coming only a month after the death of Chris Hani, would have led to considerable destabilisation. The right wing is doing what it can to force young black radicals to war against their own more moderate leaders and against whites. A civil war looms, on the scale of Bosnia or Beirut.

Threats of open war among right-wingers, should the ANC win free elections, are made frequently. The Afrikaner Weerstandsbeweging (AWB) has the capacity and ruthlessness for this. Should they link up with the black right wing in the former homelands to oppose power-sharing deals between the National Party and ANC, a consummate force would be established.

Inkatha, one possible ally, has itself a considerable reputation for violence, as witnessed by the conflict in Natal. Recently General Tienie Groenewald, a former member of the security forces and reputed to be one of the leading organisers behind such a coalition, warned that there were nearly a quarter-of-a-million Afrikaners armed and ready 'to prevent the ANC from creating a socialist people's republic in South Africa' (*The Sunday Times*, 7 March 1993).

Thus, containment of right-wing violence is critical to the transition, requiring steps to deal with the causes of political violence (as discussed by Johan Olivier in Chapter 1), the ending of the Natal conflict (as discussed by Rupert Taylor and Mark Shaw in Chapter 2), and reform of the police to ensure impartiality in police practice and serious effort to deal with right-wingers (as discussed by Ronald Weitzer in Chapter 4).

However, violence does not only arise from the right wing. Left-wingers, mostly young black radicals connected with para-military organisations, have undertaken random and indiscriminate attacks on whites. Innocent whites drinking in a bar were shot dead in East London in 1993. Attacks on isolated white farmers, intended to drive them off the land, are common. These attacks feed right-wing fears, and need to be prevented if insecurities are not be exaggerated among moderate whites. If they are not prevented, the conflagration will darken the dawn. As Robert Schrire points out (1992: p. 141), high levels of violence pose three types of danger to fundamental change. High levels of violence may harden attitudes to the point that a political settlement becomes impossible to negotiate. Secondly, violence would polarise people in South Africa, so that parties to a negotiated settlement could not persuade their constituencies of the value of compromise. Finally, violence will destroy the fabric of society to the extent that it disintegrates and militant groups make the country ungovernable.

Gunmen from all sides, therefore, must be isolated politically by all responsible politicians, and pursued ruthlessly by the police. Even so, as Olivier points out in Chapter 1, a political settlement is unlikely to end the violence. But if a political settlement does not guarantee a peaceful outcome, as others agree (Maré, 1992; Schrire, 1992: p. 142), it will ensure that violence loses popular support when directed against a legitimate government. Under these conditions violence is likely to be reduced in scale and frequency. A successful constitutional settlement thus becomes an important factor in peace, demonstrating once and for all to unreconstructed racists that apartheid is dead and cannot be resurrected, and that violence cannot bring about any alternative to democratisation.

Another of the problems of the transition, therefore, is the failure to achieve a speedy constitutional settlement. While the formulation of a final constitutional settlement should not be rushed (Giliomee and Schlemmer, 1989: p. 247), neither should it be unnecessarily delayed. Negotiation perforce requires a willingness to accept a second-best political solution, and some of the parties to the negotiation show no readiness to do this at the present juncture. As Kierin O'Malley argues in Chapter 6, there is no agreement among negotiators about the meaning of democracy or the structures to realise it. This might simply represent the different positional stances taken in the bargaining stage, and there has been some shift toward the centre amongst the ANC and National Party. The ANC, for example, advocates a unitary state and majority rule, but in its constitutional proposals issued in April 1991, it also accepts the desirability of a Bill of Rights, strong local government and control over executive power. The National Party, as O'Malley emphasises, has moved away considerably from its former support for ethnic politics. However, differences remain and at some point or other, political parties need to adopt interests which put the new South Africa above sectional interests. In this sense, it is important for right-wingers to see that a negotiated settlement will be underwritten internationally, as Adrian Guelke discusses in Chapter 7 on external mediation. But it will also need to be underwritten by the mass of moderate South Africans, black and white, supported by a reformed police and security force, such that the lunatic fringe becomes marginal to the political process, even if its violence continues in the short term. A speedy political settlement is important in the reduction of the scale and level of violence by marginalising the violence of the minority who oppose it.

But another factor is important if violence is to diminish after a successful constitutional deal: the parties to it must be able to sell the settlement to their constituencies, and take most with them into the compromise. Since most whites now accept the reality of a black government, and only worry over what sort of government it proves to be, white fears about the future need to be addressed by the ANC. The ANC needs to demonstrate that a majority-based government will be fundamentally democratic, and that the enormous socio-economic problems it will face, coupled perhaps with regional and ethnic dissent, will not lessen its commitment to democracy and justice (compare with Giliomee and Schlemmer, 1989: p. 243). But whites also need to be persuaded by the National Party into recognising the need for massive socio-economic redistribution. In this last respect, the new government must ensure that once the formal mechanisms of political democracy are established, democratisation means the winning of freedom from poverty, disease, unemployment, poor schooling, bad housing, illiteracy, homelessness, crime and disorder. Only in this way can the new government hope to sell the constitutional deal to the majority of blacks.

This points to another of the problems for transition: the economic costs of restructuring South Africa. South Africa's economic growth is poor and inadequate to meet the increasing political and social demands made of the economy. Population growth is part of the problem. In 1989, for example, there was one black birth every 28 seconds, and one white birth every twelve minutes (du Preez, 1992: p. 9). The African population is expected to rise from 23.9 million in 1985 to 36.2 million in 2000 (Bethlehem, 1988: pp. 31–51), many of whom will move to the urban areas in search of work. Bethlehem further projects that the unemployment rate in the year 2000 will be 55 per cent of the economically active population or 9.8 million (p. 42). A slow-down in population growth and an increase in economic growth are therefore vital to the new South Africa (Benjamin, 1992: p. 12, argues that this is true for Southern Africa as a region).

However, the economic benefits of a political settlement could be enormous, as the South African economy becomes the regional powerhouse and stimulates further economic activity in South Africa (see Spicer and Reichardt, 1992: p. 273). However, Spicer and Reichardt (1992: p. 266) also point out that international economic goodwill may be limited because of the other drains on Western economic aid caused by the end of the Cold War and the need economically to underwrite political and economic liberalisation in the former communist bloc.

Nonetheless, a legitimate political settlement could see renewed international investment in South Africa; how ironic, then, with sanctions soon to go, that the instability caused by continued political violence could frighten overseas investors away. There is an economic gain to be made, in other words, from peace, which will hopefully bear forcibly upon the minds of all South Africans. Johnson estimated, for example, that sanctions would have cost South Africa two million jobs by the year 2000, concentrated heavily in the unskilled category, which mainly employs blacks (1990: p. 104). A legitimate political settlement that negates the need for sanctions therefore also clearly has economic gains.

Yet while restructuring inevitably means greater economic opportunities for black South Africans, it brings less economic protection for whites. Unemployment is part of white fears of the future: but then few other societies have so protected the employment of white workers. But the sight of white beggars, found in most large cities, and even squatter camps for homeless and jobless whites (as exist, for example, in Richards Bay), needs some adjustment in the psyche of whites. The nationwide charity Operation Hunger estimated in 1993 that it gave free food to 100 000 whites. Yet this relative impoverishment must be understood by whites as the inevitable consequence of the ending of their special economic protection, and that to continue special protection through apartheid practices would bring greater economic costs.

Economic restructuring is important to another problem of the transition, which is lawlessness, crime and disorder. As John D. Brewer points out in Chapter 3, crime levels have soared in South Africa, although this is primarily due to the crime generic tendencies of South African society rather than reform itself. However, Brewer does emphasise that reform has changed some of the dynamics of crime. Crimes against wealthy blacks are now common, some committed by poor whites, which means that some black South Africans are now beginning to take protection measures by attending self-defence classes and purchasing guns: the high level of crime causes as much concern to law-abiding blacks as to whites. For every day of the month in April 1992, for example, there were 139 armed robberies, 190 cases of car theft, and 206 cases of burglary from business premises, 342 from white residential homes and 189 from black residential homes (du Preez, 1992: pp. 4–5). In the first four months of the year in 1992, there were an average of just over 51 murders each day. The number of rapes ran at an average of 80 cases a day (du Preez, 1992: p. 3).

Crime at this level feeds people's insecurities and fears about the future and needs to be reduced if stability is to be restored. This can be done by a reform in police practice to focus greater effort and resource on ordinary crime-fighting, which has never been a major interest before because of the emphasis on political policing (see Weitzer in this volume; also see Brewer, 1994); the development of a legitimate police force to ensure a partnership between the police and public in the fight against crime; and a more equitable redistribution of socio-economic resources and life-chances so that crime is no longer a rational form of economic survival for many blacks. In this regard, the expansion in economic growth is vital to the crime problem.

Education is also important in reducing crime. The provision of better schooling for blacks by means of educational desegregation becomes critical to the expansion of life-chance opportunities for young blacks, as discussed by Anthony Lemon in Chapter 5. He illustrates the ambivalence to educational reform shown so far, which does not bode well for the future. Yet improvements in educational provision are important for future stability. Some way must also be found to cater for the educational needs of those youngsters who went through the system during the 1980s when education was politicised and their training disrupted, leaving school often with no qualifications and little formal education. These are the youngsters who roam the streets of townships in criminal gangs, sometimes now harassing the privileged section of younger black schoolchildren who, since reform, have the opportunity to attend private schools in white areas in far greater numbers.

This example identifies another problem of transition, which is the failure of reform to proceed quickly or far enough to satisfy the majority of moderate opinion. Educational desegregation and police reform are but two instances discussed in this volume. The National Party government seems to be doing what it can to delay educational desegregation, and the police still appear trigger-happy and partisan, although they acted effectively in uncovering the conspiracy behind Chris Hani's assassination. Above all, however, the vacuum left by delays in political reform breeds insecurity, and it is incumbent on all participants to proceed apace in finding a political settlement. This is true of the government and all other participants to the negotiations, who should continue to discuss a constitutional settlement rather than engage in symbolic walk-outs. Admittedly, leaders need to bring followers with them in any agreed settlement in order for it to be legitimate and stable, and extremists within each constituency are causing leaders to delay, but the vacuum of indecision at the top also causes instability. A quick move to majority rule, free elections and a constitutional deal seems imperative if the instability of the transition is not to have long-term effects on the new South Africa.

One of the greatest problems, however, emphasised by O'Malley in Chapter 6, is that there is little political agreement. This is why the negotiations are taking so long and the transitional period is becoming so problematic. The white and black right wings seek a confederal system, allowing a Boer state and ethnic statelets for the former Bantustan leaders. General Groenewald's preferred option, for example, is to divide South Africa into thirteen states on ethnic lines, each with its own taxation, constitution and defence force, while a central body would only oversee national utilities like water and electricity. The Boer volkstaat would embrace much of Transvaal and the northern Orange Free State, but would exclude the Witwatersrand, which contains the gold mines and about half of South Africa's industrial capacity. The National Party, as O'Malley emphasises in Chapter 6, has abandoned separate development but still wants a constitutional deal which reserves for whites a significant role in power-sharing. The ANC, however, wants a unitary state. However, the ANC is itself divided about its preferred regime model within a unitary state, and open conflict is emerging within its ranks. Mandela's appeals for peace have been shouted down by younger radicals. Accusations and counter-accusations have resulted in allegations from ANC quarters that an opposed faction within the ANC helped set up Chris Hani for assassination, that Nelson Mandela will die of lung disease during 1993, and that Winnie

Mandela, a leading supporter of Hani, is mentally ill and should be hospitalised. The problems of transition, however, caused by uncertainty, delay and indecision, require that a settlement be negotiated soon despite these differences.

Nonetheless, small steps have been taken and the political landscape of South Africa is changing, with both major parties moving toward the centre and trying to mobilise support on a non-racial basis. The National Party, for example, has activists working in the townships and the ANC in the smart white suburbs. It cannot be assumed that the National Party has an exclusive white constituency, nor the ANC solely a black vote. There is also some uncertainty that the ANC will win the first free election by the expected landslide, forcing it to act politically to mobilise support rather than rely on race-based loyalties alone.

This points to one of the ways in which ethnicity is being depoliticised; another of the problems of the transition is that it is not depoliticised enough. In as much as apartheid depended on forced ethnic identities, its abolition has been heralded as the end of ethnicity in South Africa. Ethnic identities, however, are psychologically important to some group members and the apartheid of the mind cannot be so easily overturned in people's psyche. But whether or not old ethnic identities persist in the new South Africa is less important than the political use and misuse made of ethnicity. As Maré shows (1992), apartheid manipulated ethnicity as a means of political mobilisation in the competition for political power and privilege. This was true of homeland leaders also. Buthelezi and Inkatha, for example, had mobilising strategies, symbols, agents and structures made available by apartheid policy and the homeland system (the example of Inkatha is discussed by Maré, 1992: pp. 52–104). Yet ethnic identity or self-conscious membership of an ethnic group are not automatically or inherently political acts, and need not be the basis of political mobilisation. If ethnicity was divorced from political mobilisation, politics would not have to entail the manipulation and fanning of ethnic sentiments (Maré, 1992: p. 107).

The new South Africa will be a more stable and peaceful society if such a separation occurs; violence and instability will persist, in the transitional period and beyond, while group identities define political practice and strategies. Maré shows how this divorce could be arranged in the new South Africa by developing a constitution which did not enshrine ethnic blocs, by defining rights in a Bill of Rights on individual rather than group terms, the development of a whole range of intermediate organisations which mediate political interests, such as women's groups, sports bodies, churches and the like, and a necessary shift in mind-set and practice among the major parties away from ethnic politics (1992: p. 108). The ANC and National Party appear to be doing this as free elections loom; the problem remains that of the right wings, black and white, whose sole political base is ethnic identity. What role they choose to adopt in the new South Africa, that of spoiler or reluctant player, will be a large determinant of how far the country proceeds beyond midnight.

CONCLUSION

This is not the place to dictate what constitutional arrangement should emerge from the negotiation process, save that it be one which is legitimate and holds widespread support; save also that it is made clear to all South Africans that constitutional rearrangements are not the end of the restructuring. The task of reconstruction must also address housing needs, health provision, education, employment, policing, criminal justice and penal policy, crime prevention and detection, and freedom from violence and random killing. The task of reconstruction, in other words, will not end with a political settlement but only really begin then. Thus black South Africans must accept that their aspirations and expectations of the new South Africa have to be sorely limited by circumstance and opportunity. This, in fact, will probably prove to be the biggest problem of transition – lowering people's expectations of the new South Africa. The new South Africa has taken, after all, only a few small steps on what is a very long journey to reconstruction, and cannot be expected to be at its destination so soon after setting off. Political democratisation is a stage in the process of reconstruction, not the end point.

But so as not to close this review of the problems of transition on a pessimistic note, it is worth recalling that the darkest time is often just before dawn, and when it comes the sun rises quickly. A negotiated constitutional settlement and free elections may well initiate a speedier enlightenment for the new South Africa than is currently envisioned.

BIBLIOGRAPHY

Benjamin, L. 1992. 'Southern Africa: The Moment of Truth', in L. Benjamin and C. Gregory (eds), *Southern Africa at the Crossroads* (Johannesburg, Justified Press).

Bethlehem, R. 1988. *Economics in a Revolutionary Society: Sanctions and the Transformation of South Africa* (Pretoria, A. D. Donker).

Brewer, J. D. 1994. *Black and Blue: Policing in South Africa* (Oxford, Clarendon Press).

Du Preez, G. 1992. 'Order and disorder in South Africa', paper presented at the annual conference of the African Studies Association in the United Kingdom, University of Stirling.

Giliomee, H. and Schlemmer, L. 1989. *From Apartheid to Nation-Building* (Cape Town, Oxford University Press).

Johnson, R. W. 1990. 'Back to the Future: Looking Back on 'How Long Will South Africa Survive?', in P. Collins (ed.), *Thinking About South Africa* (London, Harvester Wheatsheaf).

Maré, G. 1992. *Ethnicity and Politics in South Africa* (London, Zed Press).

Schrire, R. 1992. *Adapt or Die: The End of White Politics in South Africa* (London, C. Hurst).

Spicer, M. and Reichardt, M. 1992. 'Southern Africa: The International Community and Economic Development in the 1990s', in L. Benjamin and C. Gregory (eds), *Southern Africa at the Crossroads* (Johannesburg, Justified Press).

1 Political Violence
Johan Olivier

INTRODUCTION

The competition for scarce resources is probably one of the key driving forces in society. This is equally true for the market place as it is in politics. Political power is *the* scarcest resource in human society – those individuals or groups who control political power control access to most, if not all of society's life chances. It is therefore no surprise that struggles for political power have been the most violent struggles in the history of humanity.

Political conflict has been an integral part of South African history for many centuries. Much of this conflict centred around access to and control of political power. The arrival of European settlers during the seventeenth century introduced a new dimension to this conflict in South Africa. South Africa's history during the period after the arrival of the Europeans and leading up to the end of the nineteenth century was characterised by an intensified struggle for political control of this region. This struggle had two components. First, the subjugation of the African population by the Europeans through their superior technology and secondly, a struggle for political control among Europeans themselves. It was not until the late nineteenth century and especially since the beginning of the twentieth century that the African population and the non-European immigrants who arrived during the latter part of the previous century, began actively to resist the political (and economic) domination by individuals of European descent. This resistance increased during the 1950s and became particularly intense from the early 1970s. Political conflict has reached unprecedented levels during the last two decades as levels of political competition have significantly increased.

The scope of this conflict, measured by the number of incidents and its direct consequences, is enormous. Official statistics suggest that close to 90 000 incidents of civil unrest occurred during the period September 1984 to December 1992.

15

Closer examination of these statistics shows that there was substantial variation in the incidence of civil unrest during this period. After a significant decrease in the number of incidents after May 1986, the number of incidents again increased sharply after July 1989. More than 31 700 vehicles and 15 000 houses and other buildings were destroyed or damaged, 19 340 individuals were injured and 9392 people died in incidents of civil unrest between September 1984 and July 1992. These statistics are generally regarded as conservative. The South African Institute of Race Relations estimates that 8577 people died in political violence during the period September 1984 to October 1990 (Safro, 1990). Research by the Human Rights Commission suggests that 6375 people lost their lives and 13 380 more were injured in unrest-related incidents between February 1990 and June 1992. Statistics compiled by various institutions suggest that while there has been a decrease in the number of violent incidents during 1991 and 1992, the number of deaths and injuries per incident increased significantly during the same period. More than fifty massacres with an average of 25 deaths per incident have been recorded since July 1990. Boipatong, Phola Park, Thokoza, Zonkiziswe, Trust Feed, Sebokeng, Crossroads and Bisho are just a few names of past flashpoints. While much of the past violence has been restricted to black townships, violent attacks on white civilians have increased during the past year. Similarly, incidents where black civilians have been attacked by white civilians are also on the increase. This suggests that political violence in South Africa has increasing ethnic/racial overtones.

The economic, social and political cost of the violence is enormous. While one cannot put a value on a human life, the direct costs of the protracted civil unrest run into billions of Rands. It has been estimated that rent boycotts in the Transvaal alone have cost the country one billion Rands (Jeffery, 1991). Estimates have it that insurance claims in Natal and the Pretoria–Witwatersrand–Vaal Triangle area during 1989–90 came to R51m and R32m respectively. The continued unrest had a negative impact on all sectors of the South African economy – including black business. Profits in the black taxi industry are down by 25 per cent and the black building industry has also been hard hit. Likewise, the informal sector did not escape the effects of the violence. Concern among black business is such that the National African Federated Chambers of Commerce (NAFCOC) commissioned an investigation into the plight of black business.

No country can afford the negative effects of continued violence – especially not South Africa. Continued violence will not only have a negative impact on the negotiation process in South Africa, but it also discourages foreign investment in the country. The impact of continued violence on the South African economy could well be more severe than the economic sanctions imposed on South Africa by the international community. It is ironic that at a time when economic sanctions against South Africa are beginning to crumble, levels of violence in the country are so high that foreign investors may find it too risky to invest their money in South Africa.

Concern about the protracted violence comes from across the whole political spectrum in South Africa and from abroad. The National Peace Accord signed by nineteen political groupings in September 1991 was the first multi-party attempt to address the violence. Several structures function under the Peace Accord to address various aspects of the violence. The more significant ones are the Peace Committee and the Commission of Inquiry regarding the Prevention of Public Violence and Intimidation. International concern is also mounting. The decision by the UN, the European Community and the Commonwealth to send monitors to South Africa is indicative of this concern. But, despite all these efforts, violence continues at a high level. It is therefore not surprising that the results of a recent survey showed that only 5 per cent of the respondents were of the opinion that the Peace Accord could stop the violence. In a similar survey among top decision-makers conducted in November 1991, only 21 per cent held the view that the Peace Accord will succeed in reducing political violence. The results of a survey conducted in April 1992 suggest that the majority of South Africans (64 per cent) are of the opinion that the government has little or no control over the violence.

Regardless of whether the initiatives to address the violence come from within South Africa or from abroad, they will have no lasting effect unless the real issues are addressed head-on. As Posel (1991: p. 29) points out, 'for as long as the violence, and the fundamental factors precipitating it remain unresolved, the current process of political reform stands to be undermined'. The fact that violence continues despite various efforts to reduce it, suggests that South Africans have up to now been unsuccessful in addressing its root causes.

MANIFESTATIONS OF THE CONFLICT

Political conflict in South Africa has presented itself by way of both violent and non-violent forms of collective action. The period up to 1990 was for the most part characterised by conflict between the state and the disenfranchised majority. The repertoire of collective action during this period included protest marches, boycotts, stay-aways, labour activities and acts of violence directed against the state and/or symbols/individuals seen to represent the state. The recent period, especially since the beginning of 1990, saw the introduction of a horizontal dimension in the political conflict as more political groupings began to operate overtly in the political arena. The locus of the conflict appears to have moved primarily to those excluded from political power in South Africa. However, the state remains an important actor at various levels. While peaceful protest activities remain an important feature of the conflict, much of the present conflict presents itself through high levels of violence. The recent agreement between the South African Police (SAP), the ANC and Inkatha on procedures for mass demonstrations (Heymann, 1992) is an important development that may contribute in preventing peaceful protest activities from becoming violent.

Three manifestations of the current conflict will be highlighted here. They are the Inkatha–ANC conflict in and around hostels, the involvement of the state (and more specifically the SAP), and thirdly, the right wing. The first two are considered in greater detail in subsequent chapters, but a brief outline of their role in political violence can be provided here.

The hostel system has probably been one of the most controversial aspects of the migrant labour system. Ethnic division formed an important part in controlling the migrant labour system. Designed as single-sex living quarters for black males from rural areas working in towns and larger metropolitan areas, the hostel system had devastating effects on black family life. The extreme conditions under which hostel residents lived created several social problems, in that it forced them into informal sector activities like shebeens, prostitution and drug dealing. Tensions between hostel residents and the surrounding communities frequently resulted in overt acts of violence. These conflicts in many instances had their roots in competition for scarce resources, such as community amenities, jobs, women, and more recently, a political power base. Ethnicity has been an important contributing factor on more than one occasion.

Zulu hostel residents from Natal sided with the police during the 1976 Soweto uprising and attacked township residents with pangas and 'kieries'. The ethnic grouping of inmates became a decisive factor in the violence on the Reef after July 1990 when the Inkatha Freedom Party was formally launched in this area. Since the hostels were dominated by Zulu-speaking workers, largely from the rural areas of KwaZulu and Natal, Inkatha's recruitment campaign started with the hostels. This alienated hostel residents even more from the local communities. The net result of these developments was that 'perceptions about Zulu ethnicity became of overriding importance in the identification and mobilisation of the participants to the conflict in the Reef townships' (Minnaar *et al.*, 1992: p. 2).

In a number of Reef hostels non-Zulu residents were expelled and hostels became centres of refuge for Inkatha supporters. These hostels were used as bases from which attacks were launched against surrounding townships and squatter communities, many associated with the rival ANC. The Independent Board of Inquiry found that 261 attacks were launched from hostels on the Reef between July 1990 and April 1992. The introduction of firearms into the conflict led to a dramatic increase in fatalities. An estimated 1207 people lost their lives and 3697 were injured in these attacks. The close proximity of some of these hostels to the rail-system on the Reef contributed to the trains becoming another location for the conflict. A total number of 23 train attacks were reported between July 1990 and April 1992 which resulted in the death of 23 individuals and 277 injuries. After a brief period of peace on the trains, train attacks resumed. The Boipatong massacre of June 1992, which left more than forty people dead, stands as a grim example of the conflict between Inkatha-aligned hostel residents and the surrounding communities, aligned primarily with the ANC. Allegations of police/third force involvement in this incident have not been substantiated, although the Goldstone Commission is currently investigating the incident. In fact, the impartiality of the SAP in the political conflict has been questioned from several quarters.

The credibility of the SAP as an impartial law enforcement agency has long been seriously questioned. One of the major factors that explains this is the traditional role the SAP had to play as political agent of the apartheid state. Coupled with this are years of security legislation which gave the SAP virtually unlimited powers and created the view that they are accountable to no one – not to the courts, not to parliament, and certainly not to the public.

Deaths of political prisoners in police custody/detention and the deaths of political activists under questionable circumstances or through assassinations, suggest a close link between the SAP and the rest of the security establishment. The recent revelations by Dr Jonathan Gluckmann that post-mortems he had conducted revealed that 90 per cent of 200 deaths in detention had probably been caused by police action, sent shockwaves through South Africa. Since his revelations in July 1992, a further twelve people died in police custody up to September. The unfolding saga of the Matthew Goniwe case, in which senior government officials are alleged to have been involved, has reinforced the perception of a partisan police force. All this raises important questions about the extent to which police reform has already been instituted. Needless to say, the lack of accountability of the SAP has been identified by many as one of the key issues that explains, at least in part, misconduct by the force and its members. The establishment of structures that would facilitate accountability has until recently been virtually impossible. The great concern about the activities of the SAP and its lack of credibility among the majority of South Africans resulted in the inclusion of a Code of Conduct for the SAP in the National Peace Accord.

The protracted political conflict and the resulting violence in South Africa are probably the most important factors that can negatively affect the negotiation process. Widespread allegations of misconduct in the policing of political violence by the SAP–SADF alliance (overtly partisan activities and through various acts of omission), as well as considerable evidence that the police are provoking violence, exacerbate the situation. In fact, political violence and police misconduct have threatened to derail the negotiation process on more than one occasion. The ANC's reluctance to re-start political negotiations with the government because of the continued high levels of violence, stands as a reminder of this. One of the clearest examples of partisanship by the SAP is the well-publicised Trust Feed case. Captain Brian Mitchell collaborated with local Inkatha officials against the Trust Feed Crisis Committee (TFCC), alleged to have been ANC/UDF-aligned. This culminated in early December 1988 in the detention of some 11 TFCC members and the confiscation of weapons. Police special constables under Mitchell's command raided a house on the evening of 3 December 1988 and killed 11 people, some of whom were women and children. In subsequent court proceedings the Supreme Court found that the massacre was the final event in a joint SAP–National Security Management System operation to disrupt the Trust Feed community and to give Inkatha control over the Trust Feed settlement. Senior police officers were implicated in a cover-up attempt and the judge criticised the police's own investigation of this incident and called for a public inquiry.

An aspect closely linked to the above is the suggestion that members of the SAP and their military counterparts are actively engaged in a clandestine campaign to disrupt the negotiation process by committing acts of terror and fuelling sectarian township violence. Recent political violence has been characterised by the assassination of ANC and Inkatha officials and by a spate of what seems to be unmotivated massacres of black civilians. There is mounting evidence that right-wing elements in the security forces, generally referred to as the third force, have been responsible for perpetrating many of these acts. Former members of covert units of the military and the police have been the source of such evidence.

In order to examine the right wing, as it exists and functions within South African society today, it is necessary to indicate the parameters within which it is defined. The term is used here to refer to various groupings of people who have, as their main aim, the reinvigoration of a historically-based exclusive Afrikaner nationalism. These groupings cover all aspects of social activity, thus encompassing it in its entirety (Grobbelaar, 1991: p. 288). The first grouping represents party-political organisations and includes political parties such as the Conservative Party (CP) and the Herstigte Nasionale Party (HNP). Their main aim is to further the cause of Afrikaner nationalism via parliamentary structures. During the referendum in March 1992 they suffered a serious setback, but even so it is obvious from the figures in the metropolitan areas of the Transvaal (excluding Johannesburg) and the Orange Free State that the right wing has consolidated its support. The mean 'no' vote for these areas (Pietersburg, Pretoria, Roodepoort, Kroonstad, Bloemfontein and Kimberley) was 47.2 per cent, 15.9 per cent higher than the 31.3 per cent for the rest of the country (Grobbelaar, 1992).

The second grouping is religious organisations such as the Afrikaanse Protestante Kerk (APK). It was formed in 1987 after a split in one of the biggest Afrikaner churches, the Nederduits Gereformeerde Kerk (NGK). The moderator of the APK stated that the establishment of the APK was necessitated by the fact that the NGK introduced politics into the church. He was referring to a statement by the NGK in 1986 that apartheid was a sin (Kotzé and Greyling, 1991: p. 90). Ultra-right-wing religious organisations include the Church of the Creator and the Congregation of the Nation of the Covenant. Such organisations believe in white racial superiority and particularly that blacks cannot go to heaven. Blackness to them is a sign of Satan. The Afrikaner nation in their view is the 'lost tribe of Israel'. In addition to church organisations there are also a range of right-wing groups in civil society, including school committees, agricultural cooperatives, women's movements, youth or student organisations, trade unions, cultural organisations, and academic or research-oriented organisations such as the South Africa Bureau of Racial Affairs (SABRA). Then there are also what Grobbelaar (1992) calls policy study organisations. These include the Afrikaner Vryheidstigting (Afrikaner Freedom Foundation) and the Afrikaner Eenheidskomitee (Afrikaner Unity Committee). The Eenheidskomitee has as its main aim the formulation of policy for the right wing, for example as regards the Afrikaner volkstaat.

The third right-wing grouping is to be found in paramilitary organisations. It is important to recognise that these organisations do not exist in isolation from the other right-wing organisations mentioned above. Close links do exist in some cases. The Afrikaner-Weerstandsbeweging (AWB), led by Eugene Terre'Blanche, is the best-known paramilitary organisation. The AWB has been involved in numerous acts of violence such as bomb attacks and shootings. The SAP arrested virtually the entire AWB leadership on 28 January 1992 on charges of public violence. They are also seen as a cause for concern by many as, at the beginning of 1992, the numbers of the military wing of the AWB were estimated to be between 8000 and 10 000. The same estimate placed figures of Umkhontho we Sizwe (MK), the military wing of the ANC, at around 6000 (Hartley, 1992). Some of the other groups included here are the Wit Wolwe (perhaps best-known for the actions of Barend Strydom who killed ten people in Pretoria in 1989), and the Orde Boerevolk, whose leader Piet (Skiet) Rudolph admitted to committing acts of sabotage. Rudolph was freed from prison in March 1991, together with activists from other organisations such as the ANC (Kotzé and Greyling, 1991: p. 63).

When one considers that white South Africans used to enjoy a position of exclusive access to political and economic power, it is to be expected that not all of them would easily surrender their privileged position. Acts of resistance have taken various forms and can be classified into two broad categories. First, those activities channelled through formal political structures: here they have made use of the organisational capacity provided by political parties, churches, school committees, and cultural organisations. Many of these activities have been designed to record their opposition to socio-political changes in a peaceful manner. Second, through acts of violence directed at individuals or symbols that represent the changing political reality to which they are opposed: such acts include the planned bombing of several installations ranging from schools to beerhalls, and attacks on black civilians by white civilians who seemingly act on their own initiative. Uncertainty created by socio-political changes, coupled with high levels of crime and many well-publicised (non-political) murders of whites help to increase levels of fear and vulnerability among white communities. This has fuelled further white resistance and increased levels of mobilisation. White communities, especially those in remote rural areas that have been attacked by black individuals, are increasingly forming self-defence units (SDUs). The formation of SDUs within white communities is a direct result of an increased perception that the security forces, who in the past protected their privileged position, are now unable or unwilling to do so. The increased organisation among conservative whites increases the likelihood of retaliatory attacks on black civilians. Such attacks have in fact taken place. There is increasing evidence that conservative members and ex-members of the security forces are beginning to use their access to the state's tools of violence and repression to further their own ideals.

So far, the discussion has highlighted a number of central characteristics of political conflict and violence in South Africa. They are:

- the important role that different and changing levels of political competition play in the violence. This is not only evident from the Inkatha–ANC conflict around hostels, but also from increased right-wing activities. The present government, through various of its agencies, such as the SAP and the Defence Force, also attempts to influence the political process by destabilising opponents and thus protecting its own position;
- the role of the government in the conflict also highlights the repressive capabilities of the state in the present conflict;
- competition for other scarce resources such as housing, access to land, and jobs;
- the presence of different levels of political and social discontent throughout South African society;
- the increasing extent to which groups are mobilising on the basis of ethnic and racial solidarities; and
- the extent to which organisational capacity in both black and white communities has grown in recent years.

While the above clearly do not represent all the factors which impact on the present-day conflict and violence in South Africa, they clearly represent some of the most important. It is essential to recognise that these factors do not operate in isolation from one another. There exists a complex interrelationship between them. How do they assist in a better understanding of the violence? In other words, what explains the high levels of conflict and violence in South Africa?

IN SEARCH OF AN EXPLANATION

Many attempts have been made to answer this question. The most simplistic of these explanations presents the current violence in South Africa as so-called 'black-on-black' violence. While it should be clear from the above discussion that political violence in South Africa has many sources, it is important to point out that much of the violence up to now has been restricted to black communities. This is a characteristic of the violence – not an explanation. This and other attempts to explain the violence vary in the way in which they address the real issues and in the way in which they recognise the complexities of political conflict in South Africa. Since much research has been done in the area of political conflict and violence by social scientists, social science literature should assist us in better understanding some of the dynamics which underlie collective action generally and political violence more specifically.

While it needs to be recognised that South Africa finds itself in a period of significant socio-political change, it is also necessary to note that South Africa is not the only country experiencing significant social change at this time. The countries of the former Soviet Union as well as Central and Eastern European countries are similarly experiencing dramatic socio-political changes. As in the case of South Africa, social movements played a significant role not only in getting the process of social change in these regions under way, but also in significantly affecting the direction of change.

In recent times the study of social change has once again moved to centre-stage in sociological inquiry. Recent theoretical developments on social movements have begun to emphasise the dynamic processes which underlie movement activities. The work of Tilly (1978) and Skocpol (1979) has been particularly important in this respect. Collective violence is viewed as a natural by-product of social organisation whose forms change as the distribution of power changes. In fact, a key theoretical problem is understanding how changes in the strength of contending groups and the repressive power of a state affect collective violence and social revolution. Students of collective action and social movements have devoted much attention to the causes of collective-action events such as riots, mass protests and rebellions. Examples are the studies of Till *et al.* (1975), Paige (1975), Ragin (1979), Nielsen (1980), McAdam (1982), Tarrow (1989a, 1989b), Olzak (1986, 1987, 1989 and 1992) and Olivier (1990, 1991 and 1992), to name but a few. There is, despite this fact, little agreement among scholars on the causes and dynamics of collective action.

In its attempt to explain collective behaviour, proponents of the breakdown model, such as Gurr (1968) and Smelser (1962), perpetuate the traditional focus on explaining individual participation in collective action and social movements. They point to the importance of sudden increases in individual grievances during times of rapid social change. The 1970s saw the development of new paradigms that challenged earlier views. These new perspectives placed greater emphasis on the political and organisational determinants of movement development and less emphasis on social-psychological determinants of participation. In contrast to the earlier tradition, the new perspectives emphasised the continuities between movement and institutional actions, the rationality of actors' behaviour, the strategic problems confronted by movements, and the role of movements as agencies for social change. An important group of these new perspectives focuses on the importance of solidarity. The four perspectives that use the solidarity approach are the resource mobilisation approach, the reactive ethnicity model, the split labour market theory and the competition models of ethnic mobilisation.

In contrast with traditional views which stressed the importance of sudden increases in short-term grievances/discontent created by the structural strains of rapid social change for collective action, resource mobilisation theorists have argued that grievances are an insufficient cause of social movements, the reason being that grievances are always present (Tilly, 1978). Proponents of resource mobilisation theory claim that the generation of insurgency develops from a significant increase in the level of resources available to support collective protest activity and not from an aggregate rise in discontent among aggrieved groups. An important contribution of the resource mobilisation perspective is its view of social movements as political rather than psychological phenomena and that the outcomes of movements are determined by the larger political environment (Jenkins, 1983).

The competition model of ethnic mobilisation argues that ethnic mobilisation is a consequence of the competition between groups for resources. This model is also consistent with the more general resource mobilisation models, which argue, as we have seen above, that increased access to scarce resources results in political mobilisation and collective action. Proponents of the competition model (Barth, 1969; Nielsen, 1980; Hannan, 1979) argue that it is the creation of new competitive opportunities that provokes ethnic mobilisation. In this perspective, ethnic relations are likely to be stable when ethnic groups in a polyethnic situation occupy distinct positions in a functional division of labour or when ethnic groups are territorially separated. Stable relations are disrupted by economic changes if these changes cause formerly separated but independent ethnic groups to compete for the same rewards and resources. Hannan links ethnic identity and ethnic collective action to ecological processes and constraints. Specifically, he argues that economic and political modernisation affects ethnicity in two ways. Firstly, modernisation reduces ethnic diversity by joining 'the fates of previously unconnected populations' (1979: p. 267), thus undermining the ecological bases of ethnic diversity. Secondly, modernisation alters selection processes in such a way that large-scale cultural identities are favoured, rather than kinship, tribal or some other smaller-scale identity. This means that only larger groups can successfully challenge state authority.

In short, in contrast with the reactive-ethnicity model which argues that the greater the economic inequalities between groups, the greater the likelihood of status group solidarity and collective action, the competition model predicts that resurgences will occur precisely where the cultural division of labour breaks down and group inequalities diminish. In this the model agrees with the split labour market model (see Hannan, 1979: pp. 272–3).

It is clear from this discussion that the following variables are of key importance in our understanding of collective action activities. They are:

- the presence of discontent among sections of the population;
- a breakdown in traditional boundaries between ethnic/racial groups which increases the likelihood of collective action based on ethnic/racial solidarities;
- increased levels of competition between groups;
- increased access to resources previously not available; and
- changes in the political opportunity structure – an aspect which is closely related to variable levels of state repression.

How do these factors assist in a better understanding of political conflict in South Africa? Research results reported elsewhere (Olivier, 1990 and 1991) highlighted the interrelatedness of these factors and more specifically the following: the gradual erosion of the government's apartheid measures which enforced strict boundaries between ethnic/racial groups, the development of a favourable political opportunity structure, the dynamic relationship between repressive measures by the state and levels of collective action, a significant growth in community-based organisations in black communities, and significant and continuous economic contraction since the mid-seventies.

The past fifteen years have seen a gradual erosion of the South African government's apartheid policies which enforced tight boundaries between ethnic and racial groups. This set in motion a process of social change which is affecting South African society as a whole and impacts on social, economic and political relations. These changes have altered traditional power relations in South Africa, which in turn have changed the way in which South Africans engage themselves in political behaviour. These changes created a new political opportunity structure for insurgency (McAdam, 1982), the implications of which have been most significant in the area of political protest behaviour, particularly in the ability to mobilise. A key variable which impacts on an aggrieved group's ability to mobilise is the availability of and access to new resources. These resources may be any of a number which include improved education, an improved financial position, job advancement and, probably the most important resource, organisation.

The growth in community-based organisations in black communities since the early seventies has played an important role in enabling these communities to organise effectively. Labour unions and student organisations were of key importance. The growth in labour unions and union activities during the seventies and early eighties, as well as increased protest actions by students, have provided important organisational skills, leadership and the strengthening of networks for the development of other organisations in black communities. With the unbanning of political organisations on 2 February 1990 came the right to organise openly. This provided a further stimulus to organisational growth. During this period specific areas were targeted far more systematically than in the past, which led on the one hand to increased levels of protest, and on the other to increased levels of competition between organisations. The continued economic decline during this period led to increased demands by their constituencies on organisations such as unions and civics.

The period of economic contraction of the past two decades coupled with high levels of urbanisation exacerbated the situation and pushed levels of competition for scarce resources such as jobs, housing, and access to land, even higher. It is within these areas that levels of conflict between white and black civilians have increased. The development of informal settlements close to traditional white neighbourhoods has sparked a number of protest activities by whites and attacks on individuals living in these settlements.

The state remains a key actor in the ongoing political conflict and violence in South Africa. The South African state has attempted to counter political opposition through the introduction of various repressive measures. These measures include curtailing press freedom, the declaration of states of emergency and unrest areas, the excessive use of force by its law enforcement agencies, covert activities to destabilise political opponents, and the detention of political opponents. Research results show that some of these measures actually exacerbated the situation by causing higher levels of collective action and violence (Olivier, 1991). The political role that law enforcement agencies, and in particular the SAP, played is a key explanation of this dynamic. The depoliticisation of agencies such as the SAP is of key importance. Effective policing can only take place in a society where the police are viewed as non-partisan and legitimate by the communities they serve.

CONCLUSIONS

It is clear from the above discussion that political conflict and violence in South Africa is a complex and dynamic process which cannot be explained in terms of one or two causal factors. The argument presented here suggests that discontent, changes in the political opportunity structure, access to and competition over scarce resources (ultimately political power), are key factors in understanding conflict and violence in South Africa. It is clear that the competition over scarce resources operates at different levels and is subject to constant changes in intensity. Another related factor is the continued economic contraction which exacerbates levels of competition. Demographic trends are highly dependent on the state of the economy and affect competition not only for jobs but also for living space. Any attempt effectively to address the protracted violence in South Africa should take cognisance of the interrelationship which exists between these factors.

Will levels of violence in South Africa decrease in the future? Given the complex set of factors which impact on conflict and violence in South Africa it is clear that there is no easy solution. In fact, South Africa will be subjected to high levels of conflict for a number of years. While political competition appears to be one of the more important contributing factors at this time, it should be recognised that a political solution in itself will not lead to a decline in the level of conflict and violence in South Africa – it may in fact increase. A crucial determinant will be the extent to which such a solution will have a broad base of support. Since levels of political competition will increase as South Africa approaches an election, all things being equal, levels of violence may increase to such an extent that elections cannot take place. Such an eventuality will be countered by broad-based negotiations which will maximise the acceptability and legitimacy of the outcome. Of crucial importance will be the extent to which the outcome of the elections themselves will be accepted.

Two dynamics seem to be operating at the political level at this time. The first is centrifugal, and is drawing a fairly broad spectrum of political organisations into the social contract. The second, which is a result of the first, leads to increased polarisation at the extremes of the political spectrum. A future government will be confronted with this reality and may have to deal with high levels of conflict based on ethnic and racial solidarities from these extremes.

It is important to recognise that the South African economy is not expected to grow significantly in the foreseeable future. Economists predict an average economic growth rate of 2 to 3 per cent over the next five years. The South African population presently grows at a rate of 2.7 per cent per annum. Should the South African economy grow at the optimistic rate of 5 per cent per annum up to the end of the century, only 65 per cent of the country's labour force would find jobs. It is generally agreed that only the informal sector of the economy will be able to offer an increasing number of jobs in the next few years. This means that levels of competition for economic resources will stay high and may even increase. In other words, even though levels of political competition may decrease significantly after a political settlement, levels of economic competition may increase. Putting it differently, levels of socio-economic discontent will continue to be relatively high. This has a number of implications throughout South African society and will impact on education, demographic trends in the sub-continent, housing, job advancement, crime and ultimately, socio-political stability.

In short, relatively high levels of conflict will continue to exist in South Africa for the foreseeable future. Whether this conflict turns violent will depend on South Africa's ability to redirect the energy which develops in a conflict situation in a constructive and not a destructive way.

Note

This research was sponsored by the Anglo American and De Beers Chairman's Fund and the Human Sciences Research Council. Opinions expressed here and conclusions drawn are those of the author and not necessarily those of the sponsors. The author wishes to thank Deneys Coombe, Anthea Ki, Trevor Keith and Cathy Payze for their research assistance.

REFERENCES

Barth, Fred. 1969. *Ethnic Groups and Boundaries* (Boston, Little Brown).

Grobbelaar, J. I. 1991. 'Ultra-Right Wing Afrikaners: A Sociological Trend' (unpublished D. Lit et Phil, UNISA).

____. 1992. 'The Right Wing'. Paper presented to the HSRC conference: Perspectives on political violence in South Africa, Johannesburg, 25 August 1992.

Gurr, T. R. 1968. 'A Causal Model of Civil Strife: A comparative analysis using new indices', *American Political Science Review*, 62: 1104–24.

Hannan, M. T. 1979. 'The Dynamics of Ethnic Boundaries in Modern States', in J. W. Meyer and M. T. Hannan (eds), *National Development and the World System* (Chicago, University of Chicago Press).

Hartley, W. 1992. 'Right Wing Activists Now Outnumber MK', *Natal Witness*, 20 January.

Heymann, P. B. 1992. *Towards Peaceful Protest in South Africa* (Pretoria, Human Sciences Research Council).

Jeffery, Anthea J. 1991. 'Mass Mobilization', *Spotlight*, (Johannesburg, South African Institute of Race Relations).

Jenkins, J. Graig. 1983. 'Resource Mobilization Theory and the Study of Social Movements', *Annual Review of Sociology*, 9: 527–53.

Kotzé, H. and Greyling, A. 1991. *Political Organizations in South Africa: A–Z* (Cape Town, Tafelberg).

McAdam, Doug. 1982. *Political Process and the Development of Black Insurgency, 1930–1970* (Chicago, University of Chicago Press).

Minnaar, A., Marie Wentzel and D. Coombe. 1992. 'The "Ethnic" Factor in the Hostel Conflict on the Reef'. Paper presented at the conference on: Ethnicity, Society and Conflict in Natal, Pietermaritzburg, 14–16 September 1992.

Nielsen, François. 1980. 'The Flemish Movement in Belgium after World War II: A dynamic analysis', *American Sociological Review*, 45: 76–94.

Olivier, J. L. 1990. 'Causes of Ethnic Collective Action in the Pretoria–Witwatersrand–Vaal Triangle, 1970 to 1984', *South African Sociological Review*, 2: 89–108.

____. 1991. 'State Repression and Collective Action in South Africa', *South African Journal of Sociology*, 22: 109–117.

____. 1992. 'Dynamic Methods for Dynamic Processes: The Case of Civil Unrest in South Africa', in P. Liu and J.-T. Huang (eds), *Survey Research and Society: Methodological issues and trends* (Taipei, ROC: National Science Council).

Olzak, Susan. 1986. 'A Competition Model of Ethnic Collective Action in American Cities, 1877–1889', in Susan Olzak and Joan Nagel (eds), *Competitive Ethnic Relations* (Orlando, Fla., Academic Press).
____. 1987. 'Causes of Ethnic Conflict and Protest in Urban America, 1877–1889', *Social Science Research*, 16: 185–210.
____. 1989. 'Labour Unrest, Immigration, and Ethnic Conflict in Urban America, 1880–1914', *American Journal of Sociology*, 94: 1303–33.
____. 1992. *The Dynamics of Ethnic Competition and Conflict* (Stanford, CA, Stanford University Press).
Paige, Jeffery. 1975. *Agrarian Revolutions* (Berkeley, CA, University of California Press).
Posel, Dori. 1991. 'Violence and the Natal Economy', *Indicator South Africa*, 8: 27–30.
Ragin, Charles D. 1979. 'Ethnic Political Mobilization: The Welsh Case', *American Sociological Review*, 44: 619–35.
Safro, W. 1990. *Special Report on Violence against Black Town Councillors and Policemen* (Johannesburg, South African Institute of Race Relations).
Skocpol, Theda. 1979. *States and Social Revolutions* (Cambridge, Mass., Cambridge University Press).
Smelser, N. J. 1962. *Theory of Collective Behavior* (Englewood Cliffs, NJ, Prentice-Hall).
Tarrow, Sidney. 1989a. *Struggle, Politics, and Reform: Collective Action, Social Movements, and Cycles of Protest* (Ithaca, NY, Western Societies Program, Cornell University).
____. 1989b. *Democracy and Disorder: Protest and Politics in Italy, 1965–1975* (Oxford, Clarendon Press).
____. 1978. *From Mobilization to Revolution* (Reading, Mass., Addison-Wesley).
____. 1984. 'Social Movements and National Politics', in C. Bright and S. Harding (eds), *State-Making and Social Movements: Essays in History and Theory* (Ann Arbor, University of Michigan Press).
Tilly, Charles, Louis Tilly, and Richard Tilly. 1975. *The Rebellious Century, 1830–1930* (Cambridge, Mass., Harvard University Press).

2 The Natal Conflict

Rupert Taylor and Mark Shaw

INTRODUCTION

In the six-year period to 1992, the conflict in Natal, fought with 'sticks, spears, knives, homemade guns and automatic weapons' (Maré, 1991: p. 186), has seen over 4000 African people killed, with many more injured. It has witnessed the destruction and burning of homes, mass intimidation and created tens of thousands of refugees. In the worst-hit areas, the provision of basic welfare services – notably education and health – has all but collapsed, and it would be hard to find somebody who did not know someone who had been killed or injured in the conflict. Most accounts focus on events in and around Pietermaritzburg and the Natal Midlands from 1984 onwards and view the conflict as having spread down the Pietermaritzburg–Durban corridor and along the coast, north and south of Durban. It is unlikely, however, if the full extent of the conflict, given its pure breadth and varied nature, will ever be known; accurate figures simply do not exist.

It is clear, though, that despite the imposition of a state of emergency from 1986, the pattern of conflict has been spiralling upwards since the mid-1980s. Recorded fatalities for the Pietermaritzburg/Natal Midlands region rose from 12 in 1985 to 686 in 1989 (*Indicator SA*, 1989: p. 72; *Race Relations Survey*, 1989/90: p. 251). In September 1987 the conflict escalated: the death rate (which had not exceeded 17 per month) suddenly jumped to 60 (Oswin, 1989: p. 11). March 1990, which saw 180 fatalities, represented 'the high-water month of the war in terms of number of deaths' (Kentridge, 1990: p. 242). Peace initiatives, first started in late 1987, have been slow to get off the ground and the National Peace Accord signed in 1991 has yet to show any real effect at grassroots level in Natal (Nina, 1992). Thus, since the end of statutory apartheid in June 1991, the Natal conflict has increasingly come to play a major part in destabilising the transition to democracy.

DOMINANT INTERPRETATIONS

Initially, the dominant interpretation of the conflict, promoted by the ruling National Party, the state-controlled South African Broadcasting Corporation and commercial media, was to project the conflict in terms of it being 'black-on-black' violence. Here, the conflict has been taken to be a form of 'ethnic' fighting driven by 'primitive savagery', the result of irrational 'tribal' forces. Strongly rooted in colonial stereotypes of the 'Other' and the ideology of apartheid, such an approach does not begin accurately to explain the dynamics of the conflict (Taylor, 1991). Sociological studies show that many African people, especially in urban areas, reject 'ethnic' labelling (Mayer, 1975). In any event, the conflict is not between different 'black' groups; if such biased terms *are* accepted, it is a Zulu versus Zulu conflict. Such an explanation while being reassuring to the state, as it works to mask real causes, has increasingly been discredited and is now widely rejected by most informed commentators. Although some Cabinet ministers still speak of 'black-on-black' or 'tribal' clashes, there is today a widescale and uncritical acceptance of a political conflict interpretation of the violence. This perspective is supported by social research findings, as typified in the work of Aitchison (1989a, 1989b, 1989c) and Kentridge (1990).

Here the central argument is that the conflict is a struggle for political control of the region: 'at the heart of it lies the political struggle between Inkatha and the African National Congress/ United Democratic Front' (Linscott, 1990: p. 81). The mainstream consensus on the conflict, in the media and much academic literature, is to portray it as a power struggle between Chief Buthelezi's Inkatha movement (the Inkatha Freedom Party since 1990) and the African National Congress (including its alliance partners, the United Democratic Front [UDF] and Congress of South African Trade Unions [Cosatu]); it is seen as an Inkatha/ ANC war, with Inkatha 'vigilantes' versus ANC 'comrades'.

In some analyses, however, there has been an attempt to marry the 'ethnic' and political interpretations. Giliomee, for example, has argued that, 'it is nonsense to think one could isolate political divisions from ethnic divisions' (*The Star* [Johannesburg], 24 August 1990). Horowitz, in a similar fashion, gives the conflict a strong 'ethnic' component; viewing it as a Xhosa ANC pitted against a Zulu Inkatha (1991: pp. 72–4). The failings of such approaches are, however, not hard to see; most obviously, the ANC is an inclusive movement and has never made claims for a 'Xhosa nation' (Adam, 1990).

For the National Party, the shift towards a political interpretation has been hastened by the collapse of apartheid and the need to move away from viewing the ANC as the enemy. Nevertheless, it is important to note that (like the 'black-on-black' perspective) this interpretation is also in the interests of the state, affording it little bad publicity, enabling it to apportion blame to Inkatha and the ANC. In particular, the view that the conflict is an Inkatha/ANC clash fits neatly and all too conveniently with a reactionary 'law and order' position. By maintaining that the conflict is essentially political, the security forces justify their frequent inaction by saying that they are taking a neutral position. To avoid problems of being seen to intervene on one particular 'side', 'impartiality' is falsely equated with non-intervention. Consequently, there has been a marked pattern of the security forces stepping in when the conflict has run its course, rather than protecting people from violence (Africa Watch, 1991).

The strength of the political conflict interpretation is taken to rest on its 'fit' at the level of observable appearances. That is, the political form of the conflict reflects what people actually see and say. This is clear in Aitchison's argument that 'the political interpretation is the ... most convincing', because the evidence shows that 'political allegiances have been crucial in deciding who would live and die' (1989b: p. 547). Similarly, Kentridge's *An Unofficial War* stresses the salience of political affiliations; referring, for example, to the reality that 'you don't want to get caught wearing the wrong [T-shirts] in the wrong area' (1990: p. 23). This understanding, however, is insufficient.

In terms of the empirical evidence it presents serious problems. Quite apart from the fact that it is hard to see how the conflict is in the interests of either Inkatha or the ANC, much violence has not been carefully organised, but has assumed a spontaneous form in which it has often been far more difficult to clearly identify 'sides', 'aggressors' and 'targets' than is commonly assumed. A detailed survey undertaken by Louw, for

example, found that 'half of all violent events which occurred
... remain unexplained. In only 8.6% of cases is the cause of
conflict reported as an IFP–ANC clash' (1991: p. 44). More
generally, 'a count of those killed during [1988] showed that 62
were members of Inkatha, 126 were from the UDF and 202
were unknown' (Oswin, 1989: p. 12).

Political labels have often been too freely superimposed on
the conflict by both participants and outsiders, but especially by
political leaders. Many of the combatants do not see themselves
as politically aligned, while those who do cannot explain the
ideologies or the structures of the organisations for which they
are supposedly fighting. In one survey, for example, it was found
that 'of those respondents interviewed, a fraction over one-
quarter of the "vigilantes" and less than 20 per cent of the
"comrades" could identify the leaders of Inkatha and the UDF
respectively' (Stavrou and Crouch, 1989: p. 50). In fact, neither
the formal machinery of Inkatha nor the ANC has effective day-
to-day control at the local level. Some, such as Hirson (1991)
and Johnson (1991/92), have gone so far as to argue that in any
case there is a large degree of cross-over in the policies of
Inkatha and the ANC.

The lack of neat battle-lines is also shown in the fact that
some people, including regional leaders, have readily changed
sides and there have been inter-comrade fights and intermit-
tent violence between UDF and Black Consciousness-supporting
youth. Moreover, there have been 'attacks by Inkatha vigilantes
on ordinary members of the organization who happen to find
themselves in communities that have borne the brunt of violent
confrontations' (Tessendorf, 1991: p. 59).

In sum, the conflict is not just political in nature; to view it as
such is an over-simplification. In truth, it is far more complex.
Such empirical failings are not that surprising, for at the theoretical level the political conflict interpretation falls short. The
distinctive point is that the focus has been to try to impose an
explanation in terms of categorising participants, but to label
the conflict as 'political' is not to provide a valid 'explanation'.
This form of interpretation simply relies on the prior existence
of opposing 'sides' which are taken to exist outside of and unconnected to social processes. As such, there is no attempt to address
the underlying dynamics of the constitution of political iden-

tification in the context of specific material conditions. Just as the 'black-on-black' interpretation does not probe the constitution of ethnic identification, the political explanation is located outside the ambit of material factors. What has to be asked is why there is political rivalry in the first place.

To answer this necessitates moving beyond the 'meteoric flares and flights above' to probe the 'sub-soil' from which the conflict comes (James, 1980: p. x). To grasp the wider picture, focus must fall on the nature of the political system itself; namely, the colonial and apartheid policies of the 'white' settler regime and how it has generated underlying material conditions conducive to spawning violence. It is in this context that any solution to the violence must be found.

IMPLICATING APARTHEID

Any adequate interpretation of the conflict must be able to address the question of why the conflict has occurred where and when it has. Where exactly, in terms of its spatial patterning, has the conflict manifested itself? Here (see Figure 2.1), it is plainly evident that the violence has been concentrated in certain areas along the border of the KwaZulu homeland and on the margins of the industrialised centres along the Pietermaritzburg–Durban corridor. The key conflict locations, in order of severity, are Vulindlela/Sweetwaters, Mpumalanga, Ashdown/Imbali, Umlazi, Edendale, KwaMashu and Inanda.

It must be understood that, typically, these areas on the border are home to mass informal settlements. Thirty years ago these informal settlements were virtually non-existent; today they contain millions of people. Around Durban, the growth of informal squatter settlements has been most dramatic, such that it has often been compared to Mexico City. Estimated population numbers have risen from just 38 000 in 1963, to around 3 million today. In fact Durban is effectively surrounded by a massive squatter belt, with a density of more than six dwellings per hectare (Soni and Maharaj, 1991: p. 62).

To comprehend how these informal settlements have been created requires looking at how historically successive 'white' settler regimes have sought to divorce African people from the

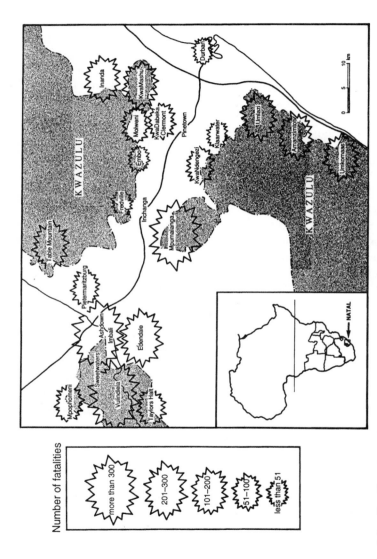

Fig. 2.1   Conflict along the Natal/KwaZulu border, Pietermaritzburg–Durban corridor, January 1985–June 1992

Sources: *Indicator SA*, 1989; *South African Conflict Monitor* (Centre for Socio-Legal Studies, University of Natal, Durban); *Area Repression Reports* (Human Rights Commission); Black Sash; Centre for Adult Education, University of Natal, Pietermaritzburg

means of production. Colonial and apartheid policies forced African people off the land into the homelands and endeavoured to keep them there. The 1913/1936 Land Acts curtailed access to land, playing a central role in the destruction of the peasantry. This in turn fostered the creation of a controlled labour force with the development of a migrant labour system and the regulated economic incorporation of an African working class. The National Party came to power in 1948 with clear intent to reverse African urbanisation. The policy of separate development led to the creation of African homelands (such as the territorially fragmented KwaZulu for Zulus) that have acted as dumping grounds to absorb surplus labour while endeavouring to freeze traditional rural society in time. Communal landholding, controlled through the decisions of Chiefs, continues to be the norm in KwaZulu.

Since 1960, two main consequences of apartheid have been at work to account for the movement of people to the border areas: massive forced removals from 'white South Africa' and migration from rural areas of KwaZulu given the destruction of the homeland economy. Since apartheid urbanisation policies worked to counter immigration into 'white South Africa', African urbanisation was bottled up within the homelands themselves, such that in the case of Durban, Haarhoff (1984) has calculated that around 63 per cent of the informal settlement population is concentrated within a 4km zone of the KwaZulu boundary, with just 14 per cent within Natal. Before the limited reforms of the 1980s, the overall level of African urbanisation in 'white South Africa' remained virtually stagnant. With the collapse of influx control, which was in reality breaking down long before its repeal in July 1986, this was no longer the case and many people moved to informal settlements in Natal. In some cases this was 'reverse migration' from established urban areas, the main intention being to gain access to land and infrastructural resources (Mabin, 1989).

In consequence, it is clear that those who have moved to, and made their homes in, the informal settlements have a range of differing backgrounds, have encountered differential life experiences and found new positions in terms of what they do now. Thus, the peri-urban areas are marked by complex patterns of socio-economic differentiation. Apartheid social engineering has worked to create massive impoverishment, but there are

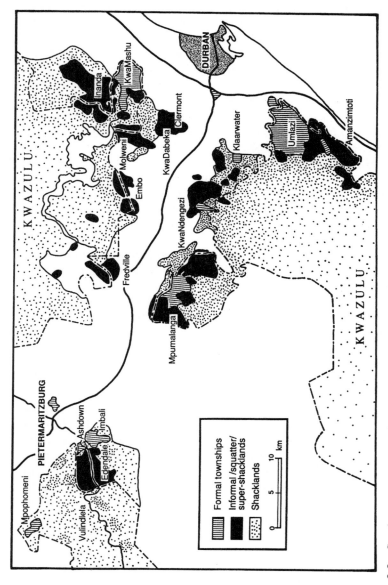

Fig. 2.2 Settlement types on the Natal/KwaZulu border, Pietermaritzburg–Durban corridor, 1988

Sources: *Daily News* (Durban), 13 June 1988; *Sunday Tribune* (Durban), 14 October 1990; Haarhoff, 1984.

substantial differences in levels of material inequality. There are those people who have jobs, relatively higher levels of income and wealth, and better-quality housing; there are those who are living from one day to the next, having little more than somewhere to shelter and are subject to serious health problems (notably tuberculosis and chronic malnutrition).

Survey findings indicate that more than two-thirds of people in the peripheral areas earn less than R200 per month, but some are receiving as much as R6400 per month (Stavrou and Shongwe, 1990; May and Rankin, 1991). Similarly, whilst in KwaZulu today a third of the population is landless, May (1987), who interviewed 1100 households in five districts within KwaZulu, found that 5 per cent control 35 per cent of the land. For most, especially in a recessionary climate, 'competition for jobs is strong, job security is non-existent, and wages are extremely low' (Pickles, 1991: p. 83). In Mpumalanga, for example, unemployment is estimated to be in the region of 50 per cent or higher and a survey of Molweni found an unemployment level of just under 40 per cent (Simpson, 1992: p. 1; Stavrou and Crouch, 1989: p. 48).

Those living in formal townships are, on average, materially better-off than those living in shack settlements; in turn they are better-off than those in rural areas of KwaZulu. Figure 2.2 broadly indicates the distinctive patterning of settlement types. In informal settlements housing costs and services are cheaper – around one-eighth of costs in formal townships (May, 1989: p. 62). And whereas there are around six people to a household in the urban townships, the figure for squatter settlements is nine (Stavrou and Shongwe, 1990: p. 52). In those areas with relatively good housing, as in Imbali, there is electricity and water, but the truth is that 'more than 70% of the African population in (Pietermaritzburg) townships live in mud houses ... [with] neither electricity nor water' (Gwala, 1989: p. 507). Furthermore, the state's policy of 'orderly urbanisation', which superseded influx control, has accentuated residential differentiation between middle-class suburbs, privately-owned township housing and shack settlements, favouring the more affluent and discriminating against the poor (Morris and Hindson, 1992: p. 45).

Thus, apartheid policies have caused impoverishment, fostered division and generated conflict. The lack of basic resources, in the context of differentiation, ever-rising population densities and economic recession, has created an explosive mix. As Stavrou and Crouch put it, 'intense forces of rapid urbanisation ... have created a classic conflict between groups ... competing for access to limited resources' (1989: p. 46). This has to date usually been interpreted in everyday, materially-based accounts in terms of 'haves' versus 'have-nots' in distinctive settlement types, with the main fault-lines of the conflict simply being linked to that of shack residents attacking neighbouring formal housing areas. Thus, 'it has become a conflict between townships and squatter camp ... between the poor and the very poor' (Hindson and Morris, 1990: p. 23). In turn, this is linked to class dynamics of political identification; the ANC having support from the more urbanised and skilled workers in better housing conditions, while Inkatha finds support from the 'lumpen and dispossessed' in squatter settlements (Hirson, 1991: p. 32; also see Murray, 1987: p. 328).

A central problem with this interpretation is that such undifferentiated settlement types do not exist. The conflict cannot be neatly correlated to varying settlement types; formal townships and informal squatter settlements are not homogeneous communities, but are best seen as internally differentiated, fragmented and divided. Political affiliation is never simply given and conflict has not just occurred between differing settlement types but also within the settlements themselves. In addition, such accounts ignore, to the extent that it does form a part of the conflict, the 'pan-class' nature of both Inkatha and the ANC. In fact, support crosses not only class but also generation, gender and regional divisions.

Where patterns of class differentiation have been discussed there is often a failure to assess the appropriateness of class analysis in the African context and seriously to consider other categories. Hindson and Morris, for example, are keen to emphasise how increasing class differentiation within the black residential areas feeds into the conflict, but do not advance their analysis beyond simply making this claim; likewise, their categories of 'the poor' and 'the very poor' are never examined closely (1990: p. 23; Morris and Hindson, 1992: p. 44). Moreover, in general, social scientific interpretations which emphasise material factors do not begin to unravel how material conditions intersect with the constitution of political identity. While several case studies have recognised the importance of rapid urbanisation and socio-economic differentiation (Stavrou and Crouch, 1989; Stavrou and Shongwe, 1989, 1990), they all fail to explain exactly *how* this has manifested itself in political conflict.

REINTERPRETING THE CONFLICT

The problem with existing materially-based accounts, therefore, is that they have tended to work with restrictive and inadequate categories of differentiation and fail to link specific interests to political identification in an analytical fashion. The reasons for this are related to problems of using classical Eurocentric class configurations rather than with the weakness or inappropriateness of a materialist analysis *per se*. In this context it must be recognised how academic work, rooted in Western models and discourse, has *represented* South African society to fit European histories and intellectual concerns. What happens is that Marxist analysis is simply and mechanistically imposed from above, rather than being seen as the starting-point for a comprehensive investigation of the details of existence, of the social forms of production and their reproduction. The point is that to prescribe such an analysis does not in itself clarify the actual patterns of the conflict.

In short, what is needed is a reconceptualisation of the social structure underlying the conflict by developing more rigorous categories of differentiation, and to rethink and establish more precise definitions among the poor and the very poor in the African context, investigating linkages to the land and sources of income. This necessitates looking beyond the confrontation between capital and labour towards the broader picture of wage labour, non-wage labour and the total sphere of production (Freund, 1988). Thus, groups who are entirely or partially tied to the capitalist wage economy need to be identified. These consist of wage labourers in large modern industries – themselves differentiated by different skill-levels and divisions, long-term migrants working both in and outside of Natal who still effectively have one foot in the rural household, and a vast number of labourers who are effectively 'frontier commuters'. The majority of the economically active population of KwaZulu, then, is employed outside the homeland. Indeed, there are only 60 000 wage-earners within KwaZulu itself, employed mainly by the KwaZulu government and staffing the bureaucracy (Gultig and Hart, 1990: p. 3).

Significant also in terms of understanding sources of cash income is what goes on in the wide range of productive activities that characterise the 'informal sector' of the economy. Routes to accumulation include petty trading, taxis and 'black market' activities (May and Stavrou, 1990; Preston-Whyte and Rogerson [eds], 1991). In fact, these processes of accumulation provide many more jobs than the 'formal' sector and 'most studies conclude that, wherever possible, individuals and households participate in both the informal and formal sectors' (May and Stavrou, 1990: p. 44). 'Informal economy' earnings are often subsidised by agricultural productivity. In KwaZulu about 500 000 people are involved in some kind of farming, but a peasantry as distinct from wage labourers cannot be identified (May, 1987).

Thus, there is a significant and diverse overlapping in the forms of economic activity. The equation is further complicated by historically conditioned varieties of land tenure – tribal tenure, occupational rights, 99-year-leasehold and in some cases freehold title – with an accompanying diversity in housing forms. A focus on the dynamics of land tenure and property arrangements, as well as on the strength of connections with traditional systems of land tenure, for example, is crucial to understanding the conflicts, both within and between settlements.

All of the above lines of differentiation and related categories have varying degrees of autonomy and different constellations of interests which underpin their potential for political mobilisation. As a way to sharpen analysis of these divisions, the starting point should be to take 'the notion of the labour process ... combined with an analysis of property relations' (Isaacman, 1990: p. 16). The categories identified can then be related to the conflict by considering how their interests have been and are represented by Inkatha and the ANC/UDF/Cosatu. In the case of Inkatha there is a need to focus on the homeland system in some detail, to show how it is implicated in the workings of KwaZulu.

As an administrative region and political structure the KwaZulu homeland has been operating for over twenty years. Today Inkatha claims between 1.8 and 2 million members and exercises power, through the allocation of resources and creation of patronage networks, at the level of regional and local government in KwaZulu. Thereby, Inkatha monopolises and controls local-level resources such as health care, pensions and schooling (Mzala, 1988). Furthermore, alongside the granting of trade licences, Inkatha dispenses KwaZulu citizenship certificates which are a requirement for the purposes of buying land or a house in KwaZulu townships. In sum, Inkatha (since its formation in 1975) has been able to offer, through collaboration and protected space within the apartheid system, advantages for some, while to others it is little more than a coercive sub-system of control – a process reinforced by the use of vigilantes and, from 1980, control of the KwaZulu Police (Maré and Hamilton, 1987; Charney, 1991).

Within KwaZulu, apart from the homeland elite and bureaucracy, Inkatha represents the interests of Chiefs and *indunas*, small-scale entrepreneurs in both 'formal' and 'informal' sectors, and 'warlords'. Both Chiefs and *indunas* are salaried civil servants paid by KwaZulu, while small-scale entrepreneurs have access to credit through the KwaZulu Finance Corporation. In the case of local 'warlords', Inkatha provides key resources and rights – as in Thomas Shabalala's Lindelani, where for example, the KwaZulu government supplies water tanks. On a micro-level, then, Inkatha maintains a hold over many of those marginalised and dispossessed people occupying squatter camps and shack settlements on the urban periphery.

Nevertheless, the KwaZulu administration has found itself unable to meet the most basic needs of more than a limited number of the region's population. This applies particularly to those outside its geographic sphere of influence and was inevitable given the weak economic state of KwaZulu, the lack of funds from Pretoria and the growing fiscal crisis of the apartheid state from 1985 (Egerö, 1991). On the ground, this has meant that some people's interests have not been represented by Inkatha. Broadly speaking, this includes the fully-employed industrial working class in the modern economy, the middle and rising professional sectors, and others who have nothing to gain from Inkatha – notably those in African townships in 'white' Natal (such as Lamontville, Chesterville, Klaarwater, Clermont and KwaDabeka).

Among those outside or excluded from Inkatha's sphere of influence, sustained ANC/UDF Cosatu organised opposition has been constrained by draconian legislation, such as the State of Emergency. The democratic movement has had to operate precariously at the level of organising around specific local issues, such as rents, schooling and transport, and in general, as Cosatu's working group on Natal violence reported in February 1989, 'the level of organisation of the democratic forces was "poor"' (Baskin, 1991: p. 339). This has meant that in practice the diversity of interests of all those opposed to the *status quo* have not been politically represented.

Overall, given the constraints that have faced both Inkatha and ANC/UDF/Cosatu structures, it is the case that people's grievances have often not been clearly channelled through any form of political organisation, and that, in reality, there is a large element of spontaneity which only comes to take on political forms over time. For many people, firmly articulated political identification takes place only after the outbreak and through the course of conflict. Thus, collective political identities should be seen as emergent features of collective action. There is a need, consequently, for a dynamic, as opposed to a static form of analysis which should be underpinned by wider considerations than merely the political and ideological beliefs of participants.

It is clear, therefore, that to view the conflict in Natal as an Inkatha/ANC war is too reductionist. Missing from the political conflict view is a deeper contextualisation of how apartheid has played a central role in creating the material conditions and patterns of differentiation which have fostered and structured the conflict. This total context must be grasped. It is important to stress, however, that this is not to deny that there is a strong political conflict element; the point is that political conflict interpretations fall short and work to obscure understanding. There is a need to move beyond the empiricist grounding of this approach and to understand the process of political affiliation and identification.

On the other hand, the problem with existing interpretations which stress material factors is their restrictive interpretation, as well as a marginalisation of the 'political'. There is a failure to probe the linkages between material and political factors. What is necessary is to look to the material conditions from which people's concerns and political ideas come. This, however, is not to see people 'as unwitting and helpless playthings of external causes' (Parekh, 1972: p. 76) and crudely read the conflict as being objectively determined. Rather, focus must fall on how political consciousness is actively constituted and reconstituted within a changing dynamic. Collective identity and its constitution must not be presumed to exist as a prior condition of political agency. There is a need to focus on the unravelling of the active constitution of political identification in the context of specific material conditions. This requires a new theoretical synthesis.

CONCLUSION

The key to resolving the conflict in Natal rests on a correct understanding of its causes but, to date, the fluid and complex dynamic of the conflict has not been fully grasped. Instead, there has been a widely-held misconception that the causes of violence are essentially political. This has led to an excessive reliance on solutions which ignore the saliency of socio-economic differentiation and the processes through which material factors foster and reinforce political affiliation. Simply to view the conflict as being between leading political groupings can only feed political rivalry and suspicion and have a negative impact on the broader negotiation process.

The way forward must rest on developing the new interpretation offered above through further research. A social scientific commission of inquiry, with wide-ranging powers to investigate the conflict, should be established. The Goldstone Commission of Inquiry on political violence, established in 1991, does not meet this need; it has been granted limited resources and has largely restricted itself to legalistic fact-finding missions aimed at identifying 'aggressors'. Alongside this, an expanded level of consciousness, which sees the conflict for what it is, should be promoted. Forms of sociological intervention which identify apartheid as the root cause, thereby countering the power of dominant interpretations, need to be explored.

Furthermore, at the level of the peace process, attempts must be made more thoroughly to penetrate micro-conflicts, expand peace structures beyond centralised points of political power and widen the organisations participating in Peace Accord structures beyond political groupings. There is also a need to create an effective central coordinating body which, while being sensitive to the root causes of the conflict, can ensure the impartial allocation of resources. Until resources are distributed by a neutral and accountable body, local Peace Accord frameworks will continue to be seen as sources of competition (Nina, 1992). Here, the provision of greater resources to local negotiation bodies on the ground is crucial, and arrangements at the national level should not hinder local negotiations but rather provide necessary mechanisms of support. As the underlying material conditions, the nature of the poor and very poor and the wider array of interests may differ from place to place, local initiatives which generate locally specific solutions should be encouraged.

More generally, the way forward rests on addressing the underlying material conditions through far-reaching structural reform and the building of non-racial democracy (Saul, 1991). Particularly pressing is the need to redistribute and provide secure tenure of land. Reform of the criminal justice system is also of key importance.

In the short term, however, the prospects for an end to the conflict are not good. At the most basic level, recognition of the deeper causes of the conflict seems some way off. Moreover, the social structural factors are firmly ingrained and, with ever-increasing urbanisation and economic stagnation, the conflict may deteriorate even further. As any new governing party will be met with massive material demands but limited resources (Tjønneland, 1992), the subsequent allocation of these resources – whether in a unitary or federal state – could be a stimulus for further violence. Central to any lasting solution are economic restructuring schemes centred around labour-intensive public sector programmes and land reform projects, but this will require massive investment from outside the country – something which is only likely to come when a new democratic constitution emerges. And yet, at the present level of conflict, it is hard to see how free and fair democratic electioneering can actually take place.

REFERENCES

Adam, H. 1990. 'Cohesion and Coercion', in H. Giliomee and J. Gagiano (eds), *The Elusive Search for Peace: South Africa, Israel and Northern Ireland* (Cape Town, Oxford University Press).

Africa Watch. 1991. *The Killings in South Africa: The Role of the Security Forces and the Response of the State, An Africa Watch Report* (New York, Washington, DC, London).

Aitchison, J. 1989a. 'The Pietermaritzburg Conflict – Experience and Analysis', Centre for Adult Education, University of Natal, Pietermaritzburg.

———. 1989b. 'The Civil War in Natal', in G. Moss and I. Obery (eds.), *South African Review 5* (Johannesburg, Ravan).

———. 1989c. 'Natal's Wastelands: The Unofficial War Goes On', *Indicator SA*, 7(1): 58–61.

Baskin, J. 1991. *Striking Back: A History of Cosatu* (Johannesburg, Ravan).

Charney, C. 1991. 'Vigilantes, Clientelism, and the South African State', *Transformation*, 16: 1–28.

Egerö, B. 1991. *South Africa's Bantustans: From Dumping Grounds to Battlefronts* (Discussion Paper 4, Nordiska Afrikainstitutet, Uppsala).

Freund, B. 1988. *The African Worker* (Cambridge, Cambridge University Press).

Gultig, J. and Hart, M. 1990. '"The World is Full of Blood": Youth, Schooling and Conflict in Pietermaritzburg, 1987–1989', *Perspectives in Education*, 11(2): 1–19.

Gwala, N. 1989. 'Political Violence and the Struggle for Control in Pietermaritzburg', *Journal of Southern African Studies*, 15(3): 508–24.

Haarhoff, E. J. 1984. 'A Spatial Analysis of African Urbanisation and Informal Settlement in Natal/KwaZulu', unpublished PhD thesis, University of Natal, Durban.

Hindson, D. and Morris, M. 1990. 'Trying to Piece Together the Peace in Natal', *Work in Progress* (Johannesburg), 69: 21–3.

Hirson, B. 1991. 'Dragons Teeth in South Africa', *Searchlight South Africa*, 2(2): 25–38.

Horowitz, D. L. 1991. *A Democratic South Africa? Constitutional Engineering in a Divided Society* (Cape Town, Oxford University Press).

Indicator SA. 1989. 'The Pietermaritzburg Peace Initiative, Data Trends September 1987–June 1991', 6(3): 72.

Isaacman, A. 1990. 'Peasants and Rural Social Protest in Africa', *African Studies Review*, 33(2): 1–120.

James, C. L. R. 1980. *The Black Jacobins: Toussaint L'Ouverture and the San Domingo Revolution* (London, Alison & Busby).

Johnson, R. W. 1991/92. 'The Inkatha Factor', *Die Suid-Afrikaan*, 36: 7–11.

Kentridge, M. 1990. *An Unofficial War: Inside the Conflict in Pietermaritzburg* (Cape Town, David Philip).

Linscott, G. 1990. 'Natal's Killing Fields', in A. de V. Minnaar *et al.*, *Conflict and Violence in Natal/KwaZulu: Historical Perspectives* (Pretoria, HSRC).

Louw, A. 1991. 'Monitoring Conflict in Natal', *Indicator SA*, 9(1): 43–5.

Mabin, A. 1989. 'Struggle for the City: Urbanisation and Political Strategies of the South African State', *Social Dynamics*, 15(1): 1–28.

Maré, G. and Hamilton, G. 1987. *An Appetite for Power: Buthelezi's Inkatha and the Politics of 'Loyal Resistance'* (Johannesburg, Ravan).

Maré, G. 1991. 'History and Dimension of the Violence in Natal: Inkatha's Role in Negotiating Political Peace', *Social Justice*, 18: 186–208.

May, J. 1987. 'Differentiation and Inequality in the Bantustans: Evidence from KwaZulu', *Social Dynamics*, 13(2): 1–13.

———. 1989. 'The Push/Pull Dynamic: Rural Poverty and Urban Migration', *Indicator SA*, 6(1/2): 59–63.

May, J. and Rankin, S. 1991. 'The Differentiation of the Urbanization Process under Apartheid', *World Development*, 19(10): 1351–65.

May, J. and Stavrou, S. 1990. 'Surviving in Shantytown: Durban's Hidden Economy', *Indicator SA*, 7(2): 43–8.

Mayer, P. 1975. 'Class, Status and Ethnicity as Perceived by Johannesburg Africans', in L. Thompson and J. Butler (eds), *Change in Contemporary South Africa* (Berkeley, University of California Press).

Morris, M. and Hindson, D. 1992. 'South Africa: Political Violence, Reform and Reconstruction', *Review of African Political Economy*, 53: 43–59.

Murray, C. 1987. 'Displaced Urbanization: South Africa's Rural Slums', *African Affairs*, 344: 311–29.

Mzala. 1988. *Gatsha Buthelezi: Chief with a Double Agenda* (London, Zed).

Nina, D. 1992. 'Slow Motion: Implementing the National Peace Accord', *Indicator SA*, 9(3): 69–72.

Oswin, B. 1989. 'Body Count, Natal', *Searchlight South Africa*, 1(2): 7–15.

Parekh, B. 1972. 'Liberal Rationality and Political Violence', in R. Benewick and T. Smith (eds), *Direct Action and Democratic Politics* (London, Allen and Unwin).

Pickles, J. 1991. 'Industrial Restructuring, Peripheral Industrialization, and Rural Development in South Africa', *Antipode*, 23(1): 68–91.

Preston-Whyte, E. and Rogerson, C. (eds) 1991. *South Africa's Informal Economy* (Cape Town, Oxford University Press).

Race Relations Survey. 1989/90. (Johannesburg, South African Institute of Race Relations).

Saul, J. 1991. 'South Africa: Between "Barbarism" and "Structural Reform"', *New Left Review*, 188: 3–44.

Simpson, S. 1992. 'Learning from Mpumalanga', *Track Two* (Cape Town), 1: 1, 4–6.

Soni, D. V. and Maharaj, B. 1991. 'Emerging Urban Forms in Rural South Africa', *Antipode*, 23(1): 47–67.

Stavrou, S. and Crouch, A. 1989. 'Molweni: Violence on the Periphery', *Indicator SA*, 6(3): 46–50.

Stavrou, S. and Shongwe, L. 1989. 'Violence on the Periphery. Part Two: The Greater Edendale Complex', *Indicator SA*, 7(1): 53–7.

Stavrou, S. and Shongwe, L. 1990. 'Underdevelopment: Natal's Formula for Conflict', *Indicator SA*, 7(2): 52–6.

Taylor, R. 1991. 'The Myth of Ethnic Division: Township Conflict on the Reef', *Race & Class*, 33(2): 1–14.

Tessendorf, H. 1991. 'The Natal Violence and its Causes', *Africa Insight*, 21(1): 57–61.

Tjønneland, E. N. 1992. *Southern Africa After Apartheid* (Chr. Michelsen Institute, Norway).

3 Crime and Control
John D. Brewer

INTRODUCTION

Three youths, one armed with a pistol, broke into a house in an expensive area of Johannesburg in October 1992. One of them was shot dead. He was killed by a pump-action shot-gun fired by the security guard: a scene reminiscent of numerous others down the decades. What was unusual on this occasion was that the wealthy house-owners were black and the robbers white. This took the police somewhat by surprise. They allegedly pulled a gun on the house-owners, thinking them part of the gang, and when they discovered that the dead man was white and the security guard black, they charged the guard with murder.

There is something deeply symbolic about this crime incident for the future of South Africa. Old patterns of wealth and power are being overturned, and this has not yet been adjusted to by everyone. South African whites, no longer cosseted by apartheid, are becoming poorer, and the small black middle class is moving in. Many unemployed whites are turning to crime in a way that has not occurred since the 1920s, and their target is often the growing number of affluent blacks. Crime is thus no longer the domain of impoverished blacks from the townships. But the explosion in white crime is but naught compared to that among blacks, most of whom remain impoverished despite wider political and constitutional reforms. This crime explosion feeds people's anxieties about the future and since most of it is perpetrated by blacks, it particularly stimulates white fears about stability and order in the new South Africa: fear of crime and fear of the future thus go together.

Crime is therefore a significant feature of South Africa's current chaos. By definition, crime is a part of social disorder, and often increases dramatically with the instability that accompanies periods of momentous political change from authoritarian rule, as the case of the crime explosion in the former Soviet Union illustrates. However, as this chapter seeks to show,

53

South Africa's crime problem is not solely linked to current disorder; South Africa society has been crime-generic in the past. In identifying some of the structural factors which explain this, the chapter ends by also considering the likely crime profile of the new South Africa following the abolition of apartheid.

CRIME AND CONTROL IN HISTORICAL PERSPECTIVE

Policing in South Africa has always been colonial in character, reflecting the colonial-like nature of society. The police were agents of the state in performing a whole range of extra-police duties, paramilitary in style, and involved in the policing of race relations in order to regulate the moral, economic and political boundaries between the races (see Brewer, 1994). Thus, police–state relations ensured close police attention on the black population, accompanied by a battery of laws and administrative rules which applied exclusively to them. South African society is crime-generic, therefore, partly because the material advancement of whites has been wholly dependent on the tight state control of blacks, defining offences exclusively their own and inculcating a mind-set in the police which saw blacks as a threat. As Turk argued (1981: p. 135), confronted by a far greater potential for trouble with the state because of the administrative offences which applied solely to them, black South Africans were at the same time monitored more closely by the police, and subject to less challengeable and more severe legal processing and penalties. So much so that the South African Police (SAP) worked against themselves by generating crime rather than effectively controlling it.

A token of this is found in the fact that, according to the SAP's official historian, only one in ten members of the SAP was involved in crime detection and investigation in 1968 (Dippenaar, 1988: p. 374). Crime patterns in South Africa reflected this distortion in police work in two ways. The pursuit of ordinary crime was made subservient to the implementation of the administrative regulations which policed the boundaries between the races, so that the most frequently committed crimes each year tended to be administrative offences (rather than ordinary crimes), such as trespass, pass offences, curfew regulations, and liquor offences. Secondly, the pursuit of ordinary crime was made subservient to crimes involving internal security, which is why the increase in these offences was usually much higher than for ordinary crime. Both these factors explain why the prosecution rate each year was always lower for whites than blacks, and actually fell from the 1930s onwards while that of blacks rose dramatically, although after 1968 the Commissioner of the SAP stopped publishing race-specific tabulations for twenty years.

But the society is also crime-generic because of the conditions in which blacks have been left to live. The enforced migrant labour system, rural poverty, family instability in black townships, the dislocation wrought by group areas, and massive black youth unemployment created high rates of violent crime, alcoholism, suicide, and drug abuse. Marks and Andersson correctly point out (1990: p. 32) that the pass-law arrests, rape, prostitution, homicides and dramatic family murders, alcoholism, and high levels of general crime among blacks are testimonies in different ways to the violence at the heart of South African society: and it has been this way from the beginning. Thus, crime is not a new problem.

South Africa's ordinary crime problem in the 1920s was predominantly connected with the massive urban migration of whites to the mining areas and the resulting 'poor white problem' among displaced Afrikaner farm labourers attracted to the towns. The geography of crime reflected this. The Witwatersrand area, for example, South Africa's industrialised and urban core, had 37.6 per cent of reported crime in 1924, but only 8.3 per cent of the country's total population (Te Water Commission, 1926: p. 89). But even then, a quarter of all 'minor crime' involved petty administrative offences by blacks intended to regulate their urbanisation and monitor their life when in towns. And as black urbanisation grew apace in the 1930s, so did police regulation of the boundaries between the races. For these reasons, ordinary crime doubled between 1926 and 1946, while population growth remained almost constant, and most crime was perpetrated by the disadvantaged and disenfranchised, who also happened to be black.

The migrant labour system, for example, a vital component of black industrialisation and urbanisation in the 1930s and 1940s, divided black families and, with such dislocation, came illegitimacy, dysfunctional behaviour, and, in the single-sex hostels, sexual deprivation, which encouraged rape, sexual assault, prostitution, homosexuality, and various other forms of sexual acts which whites considered unnatural vices, even if not, as Dunbar Moodie (1988) shows, actual sodomy, as well as alcoholism, and drug abuse (see: Beinart, 1987; Bonner, 1988). Shebeens, or drinking houses, mostly set up by African women in the urban areas who had been deserted by their husbands and who needed to care for large families, catered to the emotional and physical needs of migrants and others and encouraged the illicit liquor trade, and, in police demonology, also prostitution, even if it was not what is normally understood as prostitution (Dunbar Moodie, 1988: p. 245).

The poverty and deprivation of settled urban residents was often worse than that of migrant workers, since the market position of urban residents was always vulnerable to being undercut by the ready supply of migrants employed on cheaper wages. Unemployment particularly affected the children of urban residents, among whom crime was a severe problem, which encouraged liberal whites to establish the Johannesburg Urban Natives Juvenile Delinquency Conference in 1938 to discuss the problem.

The main expression of youthful dysfunctional behaviour was in youth gangs (for studies of specific gangs or township locations see Bonner, 1988; Guy, 1987; La Hausse, 1990; Pinnock, 1985, 1987). Youth gangs emerged in the 1930s in both the African and coloured urban townships (Nasson, 1991: p. 248), but reached their zenith in the 1950s, only to be resurrected again following the township uprisings in the mid-1980s (Scharf, 1990). While some were not criminal, and a few members used them merely as social clubs (Marks and Andersson, 1990: p. 37), most members were *tsotsis* or gangsters. By 1934, gangs had become problematic enough to the police to affect training. The Acting Commander of the Police Training Depot in Pretoria wrote to the Commissioner on 30 October 1934, recommending training in the 'scientific use of the baton' when confronted by gangs. He referred to 'an element of tough low class coloured and native people who resort to violence against the unprotected citizen and count it some feat to knock out, or mark for life with a knife cut, some isolated policeman'. The Fifth Annual Report of the South African Institute of Race Relations (SAIRR) in

1934 noted the emergence of 'native juvenile vagrants' in urban areas who came into trouble with the police because of their criminal behaviour, which it attributed to unemployment and homelessness.

Without work and schooling (on the effect of education on crime amongst black youth see Hellman, 1940; Bonner, 1988: p. 403), unemployed black youth were sucked into the gangs when forced on to the resources of the street. So prevalent and pervasive did the gangs become that the preference of employers for youngsters from the rural areas for economic reasons was reinforced by assumptions that all urban black youths were *tsotsis*, which became a self-fulfilling prophecy pulling more unemployed youth into the criminal gang culture. The gangs tried to control cinemas, and became involved in gambling, prostitution, pick-pocketing, bag-snatching, and robbing migrant workers of their pay. Fights between rival gangs over territory and women became commonplace, adding to the culture of violence that pervaded the urban townships. Most of this crime was committed against other blacks, although in the larger cities there was public outcry at the robberies and attacks on whites by black gangs. Residents in Cape Town and Durban requested that the police appoint special constables, but the police declined in order not to give the impression that the problem was getting out of control. In the coloured townships in the Cape, gangs known as the 'skolly boys' would attack white pedestrians, motorists and sailors (Rheinnallt-Jones, 1938: p. 14).

The trend towards the urbanisation of South Africa's population and crime continued after 1948, when the new National Party government came to power, resulting in an increasing concentration by the police on urban black areas. The deployment of the police throughout the Union reflected this. By 1952 39.1 per cent of the SAP's manpower was based in the Transvaal, 27.7 per cent in the Cape, 16.8 per cent in Natal, 6.3 per cent in the Orange Free State and 2.4 per cent in South West Africa. By 1954 42.1 per cent of manpower was based in the Transvaal. Both crime and the prosecution rate per thousand head of population increased markedly after 1948. In 1947–48 there was an increase in reported crime of 5.2 per cent, which increased to 49.1 per cent in 1948–49 (Dippenaar, 1988: p. 224). Between 1948 and 1952, reported crime increased by 56.9 per cent (SAP, 1952: p. 4).

The average prosecution rate per thousand head of population between 1912 and 1926 was 48.4; it was 74.2 in the years 1927–45, but was 92.8 for the period 1948–52. For 1952 it was 99.

Neither the people nor the police changed suddenly; the police did not become more efficient nor people more inherently criminal. Admittedly there were now more policemen, with an increase in actual police membership of 16.7 per cent in 1947–49, but the increase in reported crime was three times the growth in manpower. The sudden change is explained by the increase in the number of offences against which people could transgress, and the unwillingness of the police to be lenient in the operation of discretion.

On 1 January 1949, a revised list of crimes and offences came into effect which reclassified previously minor offences as serious, and identified new offences. These include *Crimen Laesae Majestatis*, promoting racial hostility between Europeans and non-Europeans, resisting and obstructing the police, opium law and regulations on habit-forming drugs, motor-vehicle ordinances, blasphemy, impersonation of police, suicide, and malicious damage to property below the value of £50 (see SAP, 1954: p. 5; Dippenaar, 1988: pp. 224–5). This demonstrates the fact that the new government tightened up on the enforcement of the administrative regulations by which the boundaries between the races were policed, and extended the control by defining new regulations.

Under apartheid, therefore, the attention of the police took a slight shift, with the balance tipping even further than it had before toward administrative offences rather than ordinary crime generally. In the black urban areas, police–public relations primarily involved the enforcement of administrative regulations rather than ordinary-crime detection and prevention. Passes and documents were checked, raids for illicit liquor conducted, and illegal squatters evicted, all while murder, rape and gangsterism flourished in the townships. The 1950s was the period when township gangs were most active. In its 1950–51 survey of race relations, the SAIRR described the 'reign of terror' in the townships: 'gangs of youths impose a reign of terror, and law-abiding people are afraid to venture out after dark'. Similar problems existed in coloured townships in the Cape, where the 'skolly' rivalled the African *tsotsi* for gangsterism (see Wollheim, 1950).

By the 1960s, black political opposition to apartheid fed the police focus on internal security to the neglect of ordinary crime, despite the fact that ordinary crime flourished. Between 1960 and 1973, there was an overall increase of 68.8 per cent in the number of offences committed for the top ten crimes of each year, compared to a 599.4 per cent increase in 'offences against the state' (worked from figures provided in the Commissioner's Annual Reports). Other statistical measures of this focus on internal security rather than ordinary crime are the rise in the SAP's expenditure on detainees, which increased by 131.1 per cent between 1961–62 and 1975–76 (worked from figures contained in the Auditor-General's Annual Reports), and the low proportion of expenditure spent on 'detective work' throughout the 1960s, for the SAP spent in proportionate terms more than twice as much on 'arms, equipment, and ammunition' than 'detective work'.

The policing of ordinary crime in the black townships was among the lowest priorities of all. The official inquiry into disturbances in Paarl in November 1963, under Justice Synman, provides a glimpse of what a police station was like in a township at this time. The Report described the station as a 'dilapidated old building with an unfenced back yard', with no accommodation for reinforcements, who had to be housed in a local hotel. There was no radio communication between the station and the district commander's office, and only one telephone in the station. Manpower shortage was critical. Stations were no better elsewhere in the district. In the entire Paarl district of 2692 square miles there were 40 men; one policeman for every 4504 inhabitants or 0.22 policemen per thousand head of population. The expansion in police manpower and expenditure that was occurring at this time no doubt helped to alleviate this eventually, but resources were selectively targeted on white areas. In 1967, for example, the Indian township of Chatsworth, near Durban, had 90 policemen for a total population of 150 000 or 0.6 policemen per thousand head of population. By 1980, the number of policemen had only risen to 110, and failed to keep up with the rise in the township's population (Poodhun, 1983: p. 186).

Thus, the police could not prevent the escalation in crime in the townships in the absence of jobs, a stable family life, rights to permanent settlement, and a legitimate civil police force. In

Soweto, for example, there were 891 murders in 1966, 1156 rapes, 7747 aggravated assaults, 8075 common assaults, and 33 489 thefts (SAIRR, 1967: p. 73). This in an area where there were 1051 regular policemen (p. 75), and, by the following year, another 443 African reserve police (SAIRR, 1968: p. 52). The problem was that this high level of police surveillance was directed toward petty administrative offences and internal security. Defeating the high level of ordinary crime was not a priority. This concerned liberal whites. The *Rand Daily Mail* ran a series of reports on ordinary crime in Soweto in February 1967, describing the gangs, racketeering, and vice. Gangs used knives to terrorise victims, leading the government to introduce the Dangerous Weapons Act in 1968, prohibiting the possession of knives in public places at set times. The Transvaal Regional Committee of the Black Sash also expressed concern about crime in the townships, urging that the SAP deploy more police-men on the beat. Writing in *Black Sash*, one of its members said: 'Logically it is the presence of policemen "on the beat" which deters criminals rather than this indiscriminate "picking up" of masses of technical offenders' (Katz, 1967: p. 16).

The police did not, however, remain entirely distant from the plight of law-abiding township residents. In 1968 they started a special plain-clothes murder and robbery squad in Soweto, en-couraged residents to join the reserve police, and senior officers made a series of public relations visits to Soweto, to be photo-graphed talking to local officers and members of the Urban Bantu Council, in an attempt to assuage fears; but crime soared. Nor was it just Soweto where crime rose. The United Party's MP for the area reported in parliament that in one weekend in Cape Town in 1973, there were 300 stabbings, 11 murders, and eight rapes (SAIRR, 1973: p. 72). The SAP reassured the an-xious that the majority of cases were solved. In 1970, for example, there was an average of 80 murders a month in Soweto, but the Chief of CID there, Colonel Gouws, said that 70 of these were solved (SAIRR, 1971: p. 75). He added that during 1970, the police made 1750 arrests in respect of the 2425 robberies re-ported, and 460 arrests for the 640 cases of reported house-breaking (p. 75).

Indeed, the prosecution rate per thousand head of population in South Africa was high. In 1961, for example, it was 100, while in 1972 it had risen to 417. In the Netherlands for that year it was 25.4, Norway 44, Sweden 61, Belgium 63.2, France 70, and England and Wales 72.5 (SAIRR, 1972: p. 86). A prosecution rate of this magnitude reflected the high level of crime in South Africa and the high number of cases the police solve, as well as the greater number of offences which South Africans could transgress against. And the fact that the prosecution rate for whites stood at 86 per thousand head of population in 1972 compared to an overall figure of 417, illustrates how each factor selectively operated against black South Africans: crime was higher in black areas, the police prosecuted more black people, and the law defined various administrative offences which only blacks could commit.

APPROACHES TO CRIME

Crime was thus essentially a black phenomenon, and van Zyl Smit (1990: pp. 4–6) shows that there were two criminological approaches to these trends. The Afrikaner nationalist tradition of criminology presented them as reflecting real differences between the races rather than artifacts of the structural location of blacks within South African society compared to whites. Thus, Afrikaner nationalist criminology explained the trends as due to deficiencies of civilisation caused by racial and cultural inferiority. Liberal whites however, located black crime in social processes, such as deprivation, poverty, unemployment and dislocation. Afrikaner nationalist criminologists explained crime by poor whites in the 1920s in terms of the same social processes, but racist notions prevented any parallel with black crime, thereby enabling them to link crime with their opposition to racial mixing. In this way, Afrikaner nationalist politicians used fear of black crime as a means to mobilise white support for segregation, making crime a significant part of the so-called 'black peril' (*swart gevaar*), without mentioning that segregation was, according to liberals, the main cause of most of the crime committed by black South Africans.

Criminological views such as these among Afrikaners explain why ordinary crime was not a priority to the state, because it was thought to be dealt with by focusing on the administrative regulations which defined the boundaries between the races and enforced segregation. Thus, one of the leading Afrikaner nationalist criminologists, J. van Heerden, Chief Bantu Affairs Commissioner, said that the causes of crime lie in social mixing in residential areas (van Heerden, 1959: p. 52). Enforcing segregation thus solved crime; the police could prevent crime, their primary function, by enforcing apartheid's race laws (noted by Bloom, 1957: p. 9; Frankel, 1980: pp. 490–1). Black South Africans were therefore caught between the *tsotsis* and the police. The thugs raised the level of fear of ordinary crime in the townships, while the police became objects of fear in enforcing race laws which did not deal with ordinary crime.

In an inquiry into disturbances at several African townships in 1949–50, for example, the commission linked unrest to the existence of the *tsotsi* gangs and attributed the blame for the gangs to social progress, not social deprivation: too many privileges rather than not enough.

> Giving natives a European education has caused the schools to impart knowledge to native youths which they can make little use of to make a living. All native youths who attend school want 'office jobs' .... It leads them to drift into gangs, to become idle, with a loosening of the social bond, and to anti-social tendencies and crime.

The cinemas were also disseminating the wrong role-models. Cowboy films shown to 'native' youths engendered violence, it was claimed, and because of their low mental capacity, 'natives' failed to grasp that crime did not pay.

However, Afrikaner nationalist criminology was never hegemonic, and L. I. Venables, Manager of Johannesburg's Municipal Native Affairs Department, countered with a liberal version of crime in Johannesburg (1951a, 1951b). Ironically, he published his account in the journal of the South African Bureau of Racial Affairs, the nationalists' 'think-tank' on race, but his views were anathema to Afrikaner nationalist criminology. Crime in the townships was attributed to social conditions, which do not prepare urban Africans for settled life. It was thus linked to unemployment; there was 80 per cent unemployment of youths aged between 15 and 20 in Pretoria, and Johannesburg had 20 000 youths unemployed (Venables, 1951a: p. 20). Venables also linked it to housing shortage, economic insecurity, the lack of recreational facilities in the townships and poor education. The migrant labour system also caused crime because it affected negatively the social cohesion of families, and increased drunkenness and social instability (1951b: p. 9). He therefore recommended the abolition of the migrant labour system with a stable, well-housed, permanent and economically satisfied urban labour force (p. 10). The control of the consumption of 'kaffir beer' also provoked crime rather than solved it (p. 11). In his account of juvenile delinquency (1951a), Venables also mentioned the effects of the high divorce rate, single–parent families, absenteeism from school, and early school-leaving (p. 15). The inadequate number of schools, and the lack of opportunity to obtain lucrative jobs were also mentioned as factors promoting youth gangs (pp. 17–18). He concluded: 'the panacea lies in such matters as improved social conditions, better opportunities industrially and commercially for natives, and possible revision of legislation affecting natives' (1951a: p. 24). Liberal criminology of this sort clearly survived under apartheid but never influenced police training; the mind-set of the police was shaped by the Afrikaner nationalist criminology taught them during training.

The commission on township disturbances during 1949–50 also linked crime to another of Afrikaner nationalism's political themes: the threat of black protest. Ordinary crime was linked to political unrest. In Afrikaner nationalist criminology, criminal gangs were thought simultaneously to be political agitators. The commission claimed that ordinary crime and political agitation were the same phenomenon, breeding in the same fertile ground. The assumed low intelligence and suggestiblity of Africans therefore made them at risk to being drawn into both criminal and political activity. The 'idle' unemployed youths who were *tsotsis* intimidated law-abiding residents into crime and political agitation. This was another reason why ordinary crime in the townships went relatively ignored: it was thought to be addressed by suppression of political activity.

Af first sight it seems paradoxical that Afrikaner nationalist criminology should also link the development of purpose-built townships under apartheid to crime prevention. The Department of Bantu Administration and Development's journal *Bantu* was seemingly very liberal in its criminological view when it wrote that 'squalor, slum conditions, and a restless society nurture crime and create criminals. Conversely, better living conditions, proper housing and a satisfied community tend to force the crime rate down' (*Bantu*, 1964: p. 279). Thus went the leading comment to the feature on Potchefstroom's new African township Ikageng. In 1954, it was claimed, no inhabitant of Klopperville felt safe: scarcely a week went by without its toll of stabbings and assaults. When residents were forcibly removed to Ikageng the same year, crime supposedly fell. The local police commander was quoted as saying that stabbings and assaults are almost unheard of in the township. 'The remedy for this crime-infected society', *Bantu* wrote, was 'the removal of the conditions which suckled the lawlessness, and to replace them by conditions for civilized living, adequate housing and recreational facilities' (p. 279); all provided in abundance in the new township. In short, apartheid's forced removals promoted crime prevention. This, of course, linked crime to social mixing, the dominant theme of Afrikaner nationalist criminology.

The following year, the journal claimed that the *tsotsi* problem was caused by giving African youths too much education – or at least an education which did not solely equip Africans for manual labour. Thus, crime in Pretoria's townships was solved, it claimed, because appropriately low educational standards were being inculcated (*Bantu*, 1965: p. 166). Black crime, in other words, was used politically both to support the government's 'self-development' process and oppose more radical reform. But for liberals, the development of new townships could not prevent the escalation in crime in the townships in the absence of jobs, a stable family life, rights to permanent settlement, and a legitimate civil police force.

CONTEMPORARY CRIME PATTERNS

Apartheid wrought a terrible cost from those who suffered under it, and the complete breakdown in social order in black areas during the liberation struggle against it in the 1980s, made worse if anything by the states of emergency which supposedly tried to deal with the disorder, led to an explosion of crime in the townships, hostels and resettlement camps, which spilled over into the prosperous white suburbs. Apartheid created a large wedge of people whose only chance of economic survival lay on the *wrong* side of the law (a point made by Scharf, 1990: p. 235), and such a structural response to inequality and impoverishment could not easily change with political reforms from 1989 onwards.

In the 1980s, when political unrest escalated, ordinary crime soared. In 1981–88, for example, the number of serious crimes (called 'offences') reported to the police rose by 22.2 per cent and minor 'law infringements' by 17.4 per cent. This was more than double the increase in the rate of population growth. Specific 'offences' rose at a faster rate. Murders, for example, increased by 31.5 per cent, rape 24.6 per cent and burglary 31.2 per cent. This translated in 1986–87 to one murder every hour, and to one women in every thousand reporting an incident of rape. In Northern Ireland, with similar ethnic and social divisions but where political unrest does not match that in South Africa, crime rose much more slowly in the four-year period following from 1988. Murders, for example, rose by only 2.7 per cent, rapes remained static, robbery rose by 13.2 per cent and burglary 15.3 per cent. Based on statistics for 'notifiable offences' in 1988–91, Northern Ireland had roughly half the level of crime per head of population than South Africa did in the period 1981–88.

It was not until 1988 that the Commissioner of the SAP resumed the practice of providing race-specific crime statistics. But the Annual Reports of the Medical Health Officer gave some insight into the race of victims of violent death. Marks and Andersson reviewed some of this data and showed that Africans are twenty times more at risk from a homicide death than whites (1990: p. 56). Figures provided by the Commissioner of the SAP in 1988 revealed, for example, that whites were victims of only 4.2 per cent of rapes and 2.8 per cent of murders. Thus, crimes on the person are predominantly on blacks. These statistics do not reveal the race of the perpetrator, but earlier research revealed that in the year up to 30 June 1978, for example, only 5.6 per cent of murders of white victims were committed by blacks, and only 5.8 per cent of white victims were raped by blacks (Brewer, 1986: p. 143). Whites were charged with six times as many inter-race murders and twenty times as many inter-race culpable homicides.

Thus, when blacks are responsible for crimes on the person, it is upon other blacks. Crimes of property, however, are committed more against whites, reflecting previous patterns of ownership and wealth in South Africa. In 1988, for example, 48.6 per cent of all burglaries were on white residential properties, compared to 24.1 on black residential properties, the rest being of business properties. It is statistics like these which give residents in some white suburbs their siege mentality under great fear of crime, reflected in various security devices, and the possession of guns and large guard dogs.

The crime problem has worsened since 1989. In the first four months of 1991, there were 5682 murders, rising by 8.5 per cent in the first four months of 1992 (Du Preez, 1992: p. 3). The 1992 figures are more than half of the total number of murders committed in the whole of 1988 but based on only a third of the time scale. In December 1990, there were 72 cases of rape reported per day. The total number for the month of December rose by 11.2 per cent in 1991–92, and there was an increase of 12.2 per cent in the number of armed robberies reported for the month of December in 1991–92 (Du Preez, 1992: pp. 3–4). Comparing the first four months of 1991 and 1992, there was an increase of 54.4 per cent in the number of passenger vehicles hijacked, and in 1989–92 the increase in the number of fraud cases reported was 38.1 per cent (Du Preez, 1992: pp. 4–5). In December 1991, there was 200 burglaries a day on business premises, 384 per day on white residential premises, and 190 per day on the residential property of blacks (Du Preez, 1992: p. 6). Looking at serious crime alone, Du Preez shows that it rose by 6.4 per cent in 1991–92, and 26.3 per cent since 1988 (Du Preez, 1992: p. 7). This is double the rise of crime in Northern Ireland for the same period.

THE FUTURE

South Africa's contemporary crime profile has significant political implications for the future. While crime is only one part of South Africa's current social disorder, it is more significant than many because it is experienced more directly by most of the population, especially whites, who are mostly immune to the chaos in black townships. The level of ordinary crime that exists in South Africa reinforces fears about the future among whites, and white insecurities about crime feed racist notions of black savagery, as well as fostering support for Afrikaner right-wing paramilitary organisations and 'hate movements'.

The commonsense notions about criminology among Afrikaner nationalists, which explain crime in terms of the cultural and racial inferiority of blacks, leave right-wing Afrikaners with no hope for a reduction of crime in the new South Africa. In this way crime becomes a political weapon in their fight against democratisation. Their explanation of crime leaves no prospect for a reduction in crime in the future, because the future, as right-wing Afrikaners see it, will not affect the racial and cultural patterns that produce it. Political democratisation will have no bearing on crime, save, perhaps, to increase rather than reduce it, by loosening, as right-wing Afrikaners see it, the last threads of law and order.

On the other hand, liberal notions of crime, which see its causes lying in social processes, proffer a reduction in crime in the future only to the extent that genuine social and economic changes are introduced and economic inequality eroded. If crime in South Africa is explained by dislocation, unemployment, and disadvantage, the abolition of apartheid must address socio-economic resources as much as political power in order for crime to be tackled effectively. Political democratisation of itself will not reduce crime; it needs to be accompanied by redistribution of wealth.

In this respect, the new South Africa's crime problems are not to be easily solved. Crime is likely to increase among poor whites, and be directed towards wealthy blacks, as the incident in October 1992 illustrates to be already happening. Moreover, the ability of the South African economy to effect redistribution seems wanting. Growth is unlikely to be great enough to satisfy people's expectations and increased demands. For example, in 1989 South Africa had one black birth every 28 seconds and one job-need every 17 seconds; there is one new housing-need every minute but one new house built every twelve minutes (Du Preez, 1992: p. 9). In 1989 alone, eleven new classrooms needed to be built daily to cope with the demand for school places among black South Africans (Du Preez, 1992: p. 9). By 1995, it has been estimated that there will be a shortfall of 3288 jobs per day; nine million job opportunities will exist for 15 million job seekers, even excluding job-hunters in the so-called independent homelands (Du Preez, 1992: p. 10). The knock-on effect of such unemployment throughout the social system is likely to be disruptive, especially for crime levels. There is little prospect of an alteration to the structural position of many new South Africans: namely, that economic survival is possible only outside the law; and most of those for whom crime is an economic necessity will be black.

However, the crime profile in the future is not entirely desperate. The restoration of political stability in the townships as a result of constitutional change may bring some social equilibrium, as will the development of a legitimate and socially acceptable police force and the cessation of violence. More jobs, better schooling, and more housing could be provided if external mediators financially underwrote the new South Africa's transition to democracy. Much depends on the extent to which leaders dampen people's socio–economic expectations during the process of democratisation; and that could be asking a lot of constituents who have experienced so much deprivation in the past. Apartheid may yet come to haunt the new South Africa with a vengeance.

BIBLIOGRAPHY

Bantu. 1964. 'Ikageng Township: Crime Hardly Ever Heard Of', *Bantu* 11:9: 279–81.

——. 1965. '*Tsotsi* Problem Almost Solved in Pretoria', *Bantu*, 12:4: 164–6.

Beinart, W. 1987. 'Worker Consciousness, Ethnic Pluralism, and Nationalism: the Experiences of a South African Migrant 1930–60' in S. Marks and S. Trapido (eds), *The Politics of Race, Class, and Nationalism in Twentieth-Century South Africa* (London, Longman), pp. 105–23.

Bloom, H. 1957. 'The SAP', *Africa South*, 2:1: 7–17.

Bonner, P. 1988. 'Family, Crime, and Political Consciousness on the East Rand', *Journal of Southern African Studies*, 14: 293–340.

Brewer, J. 1986. *After Soweto: An Unfinished Journey* (Oxford, Clarendon Press).

——. 1994. *Black and Blue: Policing in South Africa* (Oxford, Clarendon Press).

Dippenaar, M. 1988. *The History of the SAP 1913–88* (Silverton, Promedia).

Dunbar Moodie, T. 1988. 'Migrancy and Male Sexuality on the South African Goldmines', *Journal of Southern African Studies*, 14: 228–56.

Du Preez, G. 1992. 'Order and Disorder in South Africa', paper for the annual conference of the African Studies Association of the United Kingdom, University of Stirling.

Frankel, P. 1980. 'South Africa: the Politics of Police Control', *Comparative Politics*, 12: 481–99.

Guy, J. 1987. 'TheMa-Rashea', in B. Bozzoli (ed.), *Class, Community, and Conflict* (Johannesburg, Ravan Press), pp. 198–212.

Hellmann, E. 1940. *Problems of Urban Bantu Youth* (Johannesburg, SAIRR).

Katz, E. 1967. 'Mass Arrests', *Black Sash*, November: 15–16.

La Hausse, P. 1990. '"The Cows of Nangoloza": Youth Crime and Amalaita Gangs in Durban 1900–36', *Journal of Southern African Studies*, 16: 79–111.

Marks, S., and Andersson, N. 1990. 'The Epidemiology and Culture of Violence', in N. Chabani Manganyi and A. du Toit (eds), *Political Violence and the Struggle in South Africa* (London, Macmillan), pp. 29–69.

Nasson, B. 1991. 'Bobbies to Boers: Police, People, and Social Control in Cape Town', in D. Anderson and D. Killingray (eds), *Policing the Empire* (Manchester, Manchester University Press), pp. 236–54.

Pinnock, D. 1985. 'Breaking the Web: Gangs and Family Situation in Cape Town', in D. Davies and M. Slabbert (eds), *Crime and Power in South Africa* (Cape Town, David Philip), pp. 87–102.

——. 1987. 'Stone Boys and the Making of a Cape Flats Mafia', in B. Bozzoli (ed.), *Class, Community, and Conflict* (Johannesburg, Raven Press), pp. 143–65.

Poodhun, E. 1983. 'The Role of Indian Policemen in the SAP', D. Phil thesis (University of Durban–Westville).

Rheinallt-Jones, J. 1938. 'Race Relations in 1937: a South African Survey', *Race Relations*, 5: 14–19.

SAIRR. 1967. *Annual Survey of Race Relations* (Johannesburg, SAIRR).

SAIRR. 1968. *Annual Survey of Race Relations* (Johannesburg, SAIRR).

SAIRR. 1971. *Annual Survey of Race Relations* (Johannesburg, SAIRR).

SAIRR. 1972. *Annual Survey of Race Relations* (Johannesburg, SAIRR).

SAIRR. 1973. *Annual Survey of Race Relations* (Johannesburg, SAIRR).

SAP. 1952. *Annual Report of the Commissioner of the SAP* (Cape Town, Government Printer).

SAP. 1954. *Annual Report of the Commissioner of the SAP* (Cape Town, Government Printer).

Scharf, W. 1990. 'The Resurgence of Urban Street Gangs and Community Responses in Cape Town During the Late Eighties', in D. Hansson and D. van Zyl Smit (eds), *Towards Justice?* (Cape Town, Oxford University Press), pp. 232–64.

Te Water Commission. 1926. *Report of the Commission of Inquiry Appointed by His Excellency the Governor General into the Organisation of the SAP* (Cape Town, Government Printer).

Turk, A. 1981. 'The Meaning of Criminality in South Africa', *International Journal of the Sociology of Law*, 9: 123–55.

Van Heerden, J. 1959. 'The Structure and Function of the Department of Bantu Administration and Development', *Bantu*, 1:10: 50–2.

Van Zyl Smit, D. 1990. 'Introduction: Contextualizing Criminology in Contemporary South Africa', in D. Hansson and D. van Zyl Smit (eds), *Towards Justice?* (Cape Town, Oxford University Press), pp. 1–16.

Venables, L. 1951a. 'Juvenile Delinquency', *Journal of Racial Affairs*, 2:1: 12–24.

———. 1951b. 'Crime in Johannesburg', *Journal of Racial Affairs*, 2:2: 1–13.

Wollheim, O. 1950. 'The Cape Skolly', *Race Relations*, 17: 48–53.

4 Policing*

Ronald Weitzer

INTRODUCTION

The police in South Africa have a pariah status internationally, earned over the years for their highly repressive and sectarian actions against opponents of the apartheid system. But South Africa is now witnessing a remarkable and unprecedented public debate over policing, inspired by the political changes of the past three years. The need to reform the South African Police (SAP), like other institutions that maintained apartheid, is now accepted by the government. What was unthinkable a few years ago – the idea that the police force is a major part of the problem in the country – is now conceded by a regime that has taken some notable steps in the direction of reform.

Studies of police reform have focused on cases where large-scale change was fairly gradual or where modest organisational innovations have occurred. Little research has been done on societies where rapid and sweeping transformation of a police force has been attempted (for exceptions see Brewer, 1991a, Brewer, 1994). This chapter examines the principal reforms in South African policing and the factors limiting them. I argue that, while the reforms are certainly welcome, they will have relatively little impact as long as the SAP retains its prominent counter-insurgency role, acts in a sectarian fashion, and remains tied to a state that lacks popular legitimacy.

POLICE MISSION AND SUBCULTURE

A core feature of the occupational culture of the police is a sense of mission (Reiner, 1985). Policing is not simply a job, it is

* Research for this study was supported by a grant from George Washington University. A different version of the chapter appeared in *Police Studies* 16 (1993), portions of which are reprinted here by permission of Anderson Publishing Company, Cincinnati, Ohio.

also a cause. The mission may be that of providing a 'thin blue line' between civilisation and barbarism or upholding a specific kind of social order, such as liberal democracy, state socialism or a supremacist racial order. Under conditions of major societal transformation, the mission may be radically redefined, although it may take years for it to be accepted by rank-and-file officers.

In accordance with South Africa's recent social and political changes, the official mission of the SAP has been recast – from the defence of an order based on white supremacy, to neutral law enforcement in a democratising political system. This shift is furthered by the repeal of discriminatory apartheid laws, which the police were required to enforce, and by the executive's new discourse celebrating apolitical policing. President de Klerk's January 1990 speech to the SAP's top 500 officers set the tone: 'You will not be required to prevent people from gathering to gain support for their views ... We will not use you any longer as instruments to attain political goals' (*Sunday Times*, 28 January 1990). Two weeks later, the Deputy Minister of Law and Order declared in parliament (on 12 February 1991) that the police 'have been used too long by the Government to enforce apartheid laws' and 'political policy' and that they would now be 'independent' and depoliticised. These declarations stand in stark contrast to earlier claims that the police had absolutely no political role.

Senior police officers have made similar pronouncements about the need for professionalism, depoliticisation and impartial law enforcement – values that are also reflected in a new code of conduct that all police officers are required to sign. The code requires that they act with 'absolute impartiality', minimum force and give prompt and 'friendly' service to the public. In April 1990 police officers were forbidden to join political parties, apparently because of government concerns over the sizeable number of white officers who support right-wing parties.

The fact that the leadership of the force is now trumpeting a new ethos is certainly laudable, but the experiences of other societies shows just how little influence senior officers and formal instructions typically have on the everyday actions of policemen and women, who enjoy considerable autonomy and discretion in their work. What matters most is on-the-job social- isation by colleagues, who inculcate in new recruits attitudes and customs that may clash with, and supersede, formal rules. There is evidence in South Africa that a sizeable number of rank-and-file officers strongly object to the new mission, while others lack enthusiasm for it (*Argus*, 9 June 1990; *Cape Times*, 21 January 1992; *Pretoria News*, 31 January 1992). The values and beliefs of white police officers remain Afrikaner, white-supremacist, and steeped in a counter-revolutionary, securocratic ethos. In the past, this culture was conducive to authoritarian and often harsh treatment of black civilians. Today the resilience of this culture is manifested in the largely unchanged behaviour of the police in the black townships. They continue to operate with insensitivity and aggressiveness toward black residents, particularly in communities that support the African National Congress, the SAP's traditional enemy.

Some writers consider police culture the primary independent variable determining the success or failure of reform efforts, and argue that the old values and beliefs must be replaced with professional and universalistic principles. Important though police culture is, other factors also play an important role in constraining reform. An exclusive focus on culture suggests that it is independent of the larger societal context and can be reconstituted in isolation from that context. While the police are not a simple reflection of the social order in which they operate, police culture is unlikely to be reconstituted without fundamental changes in the socio-political environment. Even once the latter begins to occur, cultural lag is likely, i.e. organisational culture will lag behind societal changes. Since police do not readily abandon traditional subcultural values, it may take many years before the new ethos of universalism begins to permeate the SAP.

COMPOSITION

Ninety-five per cent of the SAP's officer corps is white and Afrikaner. Recently 19 police generals were replaced, which is desirable given the questionable calibre of many of these men, their association with the apartheid order, and the inability of some to adjust to the new order. It could also pay symbolic dividends if their replacements were seen by the public as enlightened modernisers. But many of the senior managers remaining in the force, including the present Commissioner, are hardliners who have been implicated in illegal activities or are tainted by their previous involvement in the SAP's Security Branch.

White rank-and-file officers are largely conservative Afrikaners. But 60 per cent of the rankers are black. A few of the latter are progressive, sympathising with liberal or leftist parties and enthusiastically embracing the reforms, but the vast majority seem no more progressive than their white counterparts. They have demonstrated over the years that they are not inclined to treat black civilians with sensitivity, and this is especially true for the hated black municipal police and the *kitskonstabels*, who receive less training and supervision than their regular SAP counterparts and have a terrible reputation for brutality (*Black Sash*, 1988; CIIR, 1988; Fine, 1989). One measure of the status of black police in the townships is that they have been prime targets for attack. Scores of police houses have been petrol-bombed and a large number of police have been killed or injured since the outbreak of township violence in the mid-1980s. From 1984 to 1992, 765 police officers, mostly black, were slain. Reforms in the political system and in policing since 1990 have done little or nothing to bolster the status of these cops in the townships or to make their work safer; in fact, the number killed in 1990–92 (470) was more than twice that of the previous three-year period (218).

The literature on other racially heterogeneous societies suggests that, holding all else constant, an increase in the number of police officers from the subordinate population does not necessarily result in more sensitive behaviour or markedly improve police–community relations, although their presence may have symbolic benefits and may gradually alter the ethos of a department. Police behaviour is shaped more by the nature of the police function than by officers' social backgrounds. Even if more enlightened blacks were recruited into the SAP, this arguably would do little to change police behaviour in the aggregate or inspire public confidence in the force. Similarly, psychological screening of recruits and more professional training – both of which have been introduced in South Africa recently – will have limited effect on police conduct, since that conduct is primarily a result of on-the-job socialisation by peers and the everyday demands of police work.

ACCOUNTABILITY

'Police accountability' is an elusive ideal in all modern societies, and it would be fanciful to expect that a police force could ever be rendered fully accountable to external agencies or to local communities. But meaningful mechanisms of accountability are especially important in divided societies, where the police often appear to be above the law. As late as 1990 the South African authorities were still insisting that the SAP was already sufficiently accountable – to the Ministry of Law and Order, parliament, and the courts – even if these agencies were controlled by whites. Separate bodies to review or set policies or to handle complaints against the police were simply unnecessary. An official at the Law and Order Ministry, Brigadier Leon Mellet, told me in a June 1990 interview that such bodies are the dream only of 'a small, outspoken, radical leftist group' and that it would be 'a sad day in any country when you have to have a body to police the police'. Just one year later, the need for external controls was reluctantly accepted by the regime during negotiations that resulted in the National Peace Accord. The accord provided for a Police Board composed of equal numbers of civilians and police chiefs. Purely advisory and without any powers, the Board nevertheless has some potential to make a significant contribution; it has already made recommendations on changes in training, discipline, the use of force, the handling of public order problems, and community relations. The Board's success will depend on the receptivity of its police members to proposals from the civilian side (consensus must be reached before recommendations are forwarded to the Minister). Thus far, the police members have rejected certain proposals but welcomed others that were consistent with their own preconceptions of acceptable reforms. The record of civilian advisory bodies in other countries shows that they can facilitate 'constructive engagement' with the police, but the police will resist proposals that challenge revered traditions and practices. Even boards that have formal powers may have little real influence over the police.

South Africa is also in the process of establishing special units to investigate complaints against the police. Some of the first units were composed solely of SAP officers, including former Security Branch men, but the plan is to include some civilians

(*Cape Times*, 13 November 1991; *Argus*, 15 March 1992). There is some debate in the literature on the value of complaint review mechanisms in holding police accountable for misconduct. Civilian boards have often foundered under the weight of police refusal to cooperate and many, but not all, substantiate relatively few civilian complaints. Even those that are fully independent and have an investigative role face chronic difficulties in gathering evidence and gaining police cooperation. Also common to civilian review boards is a micro-orientation, a preoccupation with individual complaints to the neglect of larger problems that generate complaints. Operating in a reactive rather than proactive manner, the boards have not attempted to remedy the faulty policies, training, supervision, etc. that give rise to behaviour that invites complaints (Goldsmith, 1991). On the other hand, the very existence of a review board is valuable. It decreases the chances that complaints will be swept under the carpet by the police and it can have symbolic value in sending a message to officers that their behaviour may come under scrutiny, which may discourage some abuses. This is certainly preferable to a system of handling complaints entirely within the police force, as the SAP has done until now, but optimism about the new complaints units, given their limited resources and powers, would be unwarranted.

The criminal courts traditionally played little effective role in punishing police officers for serious offences, such as murder and culpable homicide, and this was especially so during the troubles of the mid-1980s (Foster and Luyt, 1986; Hansson, 1989; Weitzer and Beattie, 1990). In a context where large numbers of civilians were killed by police (2201 from 1984–87), few officers were prosecuted and convicted of murder. In the past two years the courts appear to be treating police misconduct more seriously, but it remains to be seen whether this will have any deterrent effect on police criminality. A recent measure, the 1992 Further Indemnity Act, may have the opposite effect, undermining the judiciary's efforts to punish wayward officers. The Act establishes a council to review cases of political prisoners and convicted members of the security forces who claim their criminal conduct was motivated by political aims. The council can make recommendations to the President for the release of deserving individuals, who may be released without any publicity.

Until recently, commissions of inquiry into policing matters were rare events. Only one, the Kannemeyer Commission, was formed during the zenith of state repression in the mid-1980s, and its criticisms of the police (who killed 19 people at a funeral in Uitenhage in 1985) were ignored by the regime. Under pressure from the ANC, President de Klerk has shown greater willingness than his predecessors to appoint such commissions. Since 1990, inquiries have been made into allegations that assassination squads exist in the security forces (by the Harms Commission, 1990); the March 1990 killings in Sebokeng (the Goldstone Commission, 1990); the June 1992 massacre in Boipatong (the Waddington Inquiry, 1992); and the general issue of policing demonstrations (the Heymann Panel, 1992). A standing Commission on the Prevention of Public Violence and Intimidation (also known as the Goldstone Commission) grew out of the National Peace Accord; it has been very active in investigating violence on the part of political opponents and rival ethnic groups as well as controversial actions by members of the security forces. In its role as a quasi-watchdog over the police, the Commission sees itself as a 'catalyst' for transforming the SAP into a force that commands respect and cooperation (Goldstone Commission, 1992).

The commissions have made valuable criticisms of police policies and practices and some of the corrective measures advocated have been accepted and implemented by the government. They may also have some symbolic value, demonstrating that the police are no longer totally insulated from outside scrutiny. But few of the officers implicated in the investigations have been charged with offences and police behaviour on the ground has not changed substantially. Taken together, the recent reforms in the system of accountability are welcome but clearly inadequate checks on police misconduct.

POLICE–COMMUNITY RELATIONS

A fundamental problem in South Africa is that the police do not command the confidence of the majority of the public. Blacks traditionally experienced the SAP as an authoritarian force *par excellence*, one that did not hesitate to use iron-fist methods to maintain strict control over the majority of the population. Relations were coloured by deep resentment, fear, and avoidance of the police. Decades ago the Lansdown Commission (1937: pp. 69, 72) pointed to the 'mutual distrust, suspicion, and dislike' between police and the black population, who regarded the police as 'enemies and persecutors'; it also found that the police tended to act with 'arrogance' and 'unnecessary harshness' toward blacks. The gulf between the SAP and the black community only widened after the National Party's victory in 1948 (when police were obliged to enforce a host of new apartheid laws) and especially during the peak periods of state repression in 1976–77 and 1984–88.

A recent investigation by the International Commission of Jurists (1992: p. 11) referred to the 'total alienation' of blacks from the police, and it doubted that 'the force as at present structured is ever likely to convince the black population that it is capable of enforcing the law firmly, sensitively, and with constant and absolute impartiality'. 'Total alienation' is an exaggeration, but the available survey data suggest that the police do face a crisis of confidence in many black communities. A 1991 poll of 364 blacks in the Pietermaritzburg area found that only 19 per cent were content with police behaviour; 71 per cent said the police were partial in their handling of political violence; 68 per cent said the attitude of the police had worsened since the mid-1980s; 61 per cent said the police were hostile, aggressive or indifferent; and only 6 per cent found them friendly and courteous (Centre for Criminal Justice, 1991). Similar findings are reported in a survey of 498 residents of Bhongoletu, who were asked about the behaviour of *kitskonstabels*, the special black police units. Eighty per cent said the *kitskonstabels* treat township residents badly; 76 per cent had observed them behaving aggressively; 64 per cent had seen them pointing firearms at civilians; 65 per cent witnessed them assaulting someone; and 31 per cent observed them shooting without apparent reason. Fifty- six per cent said they personally had complaints against these police officers (Hofmeyr and Shefer, 1987; see also Fine, 1989).

Most analysts argue that the credibility of the SAP will not increase for the majority of the population until a new, broadly acceptable regime is installed. In the meantime, the SAP will continue to be regarded by blacks as a 'white man's force'. At first glance, this argument appears sound. Clearly the state in divided societies is a key determinant of the legitimacy of the police. Indeed, in these societies a new regime appears to be a necessary, but not sufficient, condition for police legitimation (Weitzer, 1990). Much depends, of course, on the nature of the new regime; it must have broad credibility and an interest in and capacity for institutionalising reforms in the institutions of law and order. In South Africa, therefore, it is by no means inevitable that the advent of black majority rule or a power-sharing regime will translate into a growth of popular confidence in the police. The SAP's symbolic status may be raised by such a change (at least for blacks) but police behaviour will continue to have a profound effect on public opinion, independent of the political changes. A new regime is a key, but not the only, factor shaping the prospects for police legitimation.

The problem of building popular confidence in a police force is never simple in a deeply divided society. Indeed, there are important sections of South African society whose confidence in the police will *decrease* as a result of progressive political changes. Historically, policing was not problematic for the vast majority of white South Africans, and many whites continue to hold the SAP in high regard. During the current period of reform, however, conservatives and right-wing extremists have expressed alarm over the relaxation of controls on blacks, over reforms that are 'handcuffing' the SAP, and over incidents in which police have clashed with right-wing protesters (Weitzer, 1991; pp. 261–2). Resentment has been building over alleged harassment by the security police, including surveillance and arrests of members of paramilitary organisations. In February 1991 members of the neo-Nazi Afrikaner Resistance Movement held a march protesting against the detention without trial of forty right-wingers. The illegal march was broken up by police with tear-gas and physical force, resulting in several charges of police assault. In May 1991 police in Ventersdorp fired into a large crowd of white farmers seeking to force blacks off land they had occupied illegally. Two farmers were wounded by buckshot in this unprecedented event. And in August 1991 Ventersdorp was again the scene of an altercation between police and white militants attempting to disrupt a speech by President de Klerk. Three whites were killed and fifty injured. Each incident prompted right-wing vilification of the SAP, charges that the white population is now suffering oppression in a 'police state', and threats of retaliation against the police. Though remarkable, such rapid erosion of support from a section of the dominant population is not surprising in a divided society in transition. It is precisely what one should expect where the police force is undergoing reform and where officers are instructed to act more impartially, which may result in more aggressive efforts to control unruly elements in the dominant community (Brewer 1991b; Weitzer 1987a, 1987b).

If de Klerk's policing reforms outrage right-wing whites, they also have the potential to alienate right-wing blacks. In 1991 over three times as many Inkatha supporters as ANC supporters reported being favourably impressed with the police (Centre for Criminal Justice, 1991). Recently, however, Inkatha has complained about some incidents in which police allegedly acted against the party's supporters, and in 1992 Inkatha's information centre claimed that the SAP was 'generally heavily weighted in favour of the white community or ANC supporters' (*Cape Times*, 28 August 1992). This flies in the face of the abundant evidence that the police have frequently sided with Inkatha in its attacks on the ANC (see below).

Traditionally, the SAP paid little attention to the quality of its relations with the black majority. No special initiatives were made to gauge blacks' concerns about crime and policing or to improve relations with black communities. The SAP's approach was instead one of authoritarian control of the black population. Police–community relations problems have been taken more seriously by the de Klerk regime, under pressure from progressive forces in the country. A new community relations branch is being formed in the SAP and unprecedented efforts are being made to open up dialogue with local groups; police–community forums and liaison committees were introduced in mid-1992. These are all rather modest initiatives hardly capable of markedly improving relations in a context where regular officers continue to show a 'lack of awareness' of the importance of cultivating positive relations with all communities (Waddington Inquiry, 1992: p. 46). At the same time, police–community relations are not a one-way street. Communities must be receptive to police efforts to improve relations, and in South Africa the legacy of apartheid and decades of repressive policing make it unlikely that the most embittered communities will readily participate in such ventures, or participate in a non-adversarial fashion. Many communities still feel that any cooperation with the police is tantamount to 'selling out' to the enemy; invitations to participate in liaison bodies are refused. Even if such people could be convinced to participate in liaison committees, it is doubtful whether these mechanisms would have much salutary effect since they are purely consultative and fairly rudimentary. Liaison committees in another divided society, Northern Ireland, have influenced policing practices only minimally and have had little effect on community perceptions (Walker, 1990; Weitzer, 1992). In sum, in South Africa police relations with black communities on the left are likely to improve little in the foreseeable future, and their relations with right-wing blacks and whites are likely to worsen.

The reforms outlined above are long-overdue, positive developments, but their impact on police conduct and the image of the SAP has been diluted by three conditions: manifest police partiality, counter-insurgency practices, and the larger system of white minority rule. Since I have already commented on the latter, the remainder of the chapter focuses on the other two conditions.

SECTARIAN POLICING

Approximately two-thirds of white SAP officers support right-wing political organisations, but police sympathies for white rightists pale in comparison with their active collusion with right-wing blacks. Since 1985 the police have been accused of aiding and abetting conservative black vigilantes in order to help neutralise opponents of apartheid (Haysom, 1990). In the past few years black-on-black violence has escalated to alarming levels in Natal and the Transvaal, leaving around 3000 dead per year since 1990. Most of the clashes are between supporters of the African National Congress and the Inkatha Freedom Party, and there is mounting evidence that the police have favoured Inkatha because they are fighting the security forces' traditional enemy, the ANC. The standard police response to allegations of bias is either a flat denial or a claim that it occurs only in rare, isolated instances. Occasionally, however, comments are made that appear to contradict the official line. For example, the head of the Security Branch in Pietermaritzburg, Brigadier Jac Buchner, revealed, 'at the end of last year [1987] Inkatha was in dire straits, but we came in and restored a certain sense of law and order by February' (Smith, 1992). And during the trial of seven officers accused of killing eleven persons identified with the ANC/UDF at Trust Feed in Natal, the commanding officer, Captain Brian Mitchell, explained his actions against the ANC/UDF victims as follows: 'I sympathised with Inkatha. They never made the areas ungovernable and they supported the government' (*Independent*, 28 February 1992).

Allegations of police bias or complicity in attacks by supporters of Inkatha against people identified with the ANC are legion. Investigating the December 1991 violence in the Mooi River, which claimed 19 lives, the Goldstone Commission uncovered evidence that 'strongly suggested' a police bias in favour of Inkatha (*Natal Mercury*, 8 February 1992). Inquiries by Amnesty International (1992) and Africa Watch (1991) found a 'consistent pattern' of police complicity on the side of Inkatha. The Human Rights Commission (1992) found that, out of 49 major massacres (each with at least 10 fatalities), 32 were initiated by Inkatha and in 19 the SAP was implicated in collusion. A content analysis of press reports covering 601 violent incidents on the Reef between July 1990 and July 1991 by the Community Agency for Social Enquiry found that Inkatha was the aggressor in 51 per cent, the SAP in 23 per cent, and the ANC in 7 per cent (*Sowetan*, 4 May 1992). When the police were not the principal actors, they were implicated in complicity in 107 reports of failing to disarm, escorting, assisting, arming or failing to prevent attacks by Inkatha loyalists. There were no reports of police siding with the ANC in these ways. Other observers (Grange, 1991; Powell, 1991; Powell and Anderson, 1992; Stober and Evans, 1991; Smith, 1992) have concluded that the SAP has been lax in taking preventive measures, such as searching migrant workers' hostels and commuter trains for weapons and disarming groups of Inkatha members carrying so-called 'traditional weapons', such as axes and spears. They have also declined to intervene to stop violence once it has begun or have attacked ANC supporters who were trying to defend themselves against Inkatha attackers. Some of this has been documented on videotape. After the fact, police have often failed to respond to calls for assistance, delayed their response, or conducted remarkably poor investigations; very few suspects have been arrested in connection with the attacks (*Star*, 16 August 1992).

It thus comes as no surprise that in Natal 97.8 per cent of ANC supporters but only 23.7 per cent of Inkatha supporters say the police have shown partiality during the clashes; 68.7 per cent of ANC supporters and 3.9 per cent of Inkatha supporters claimed that they had witnessed, experienced, or heard reports of partiality from sources other than the media (Centre for Criminal Justice, 1991).

In some incidents it is possible that what appears to be police complicity is actually a matter of genuine mistakes, faulty assessment of problem situations, or incompetence. An independent inquiry into one of the clashes between Inkatha and ANC supporters – Boipatong, where 46 people died on 17 June 1992 – rejected allegations of complicity and placed the blame on the incredibly incompetent actions of the police. They operated without a sound intelligence system for assessing the level of tension in the area; they reacted to the incident in an *ad hoc* fashion, without contingency plans; they were plagued by command-and-control problems (a 'failure of leadership at all levels'); and they first delayed investigating the incident and then conducted a very poor one (Waddington Inquiry, 1992).

The authorities have sometimes claimed that the police did not have the means to intervene in violent clashes, that disarming people might itself provoke violence, and that the police were afraid of being overwhelmed. These concerns have been genuine in certain instances, but questionable in others. An investigation by the International Commission of Jurists (1992: p. 16) concluded that the SAP had sufficient capacity to bring violence under control in most incidents, but lacked the will and effective leadership to do so. Moreover, vigorous measures can help to prevent clashes in the first place. On certain occasions when the police have taken steps to deter violence, they have had a good deal of success. For example, when an Internal Stability Unit of 800 men saturated Alexandra township with patrols in June 1992, the number of killings and assaults dropped substantially (Ottaway, 1992). Clearly, robust police actions (both proactive and reactive) are required in the high-violence areas to save lives and to demonstrate that the SAP is no longer inclined to enforce the law in a sectarian manner.

COUNTER-INSURGENCY POLICING

The reforms introduced in the past few years are more or less removed from the demands of a kind of policing highly conducive to abuses of power, i.e. counter-insurgency policing: the methods the SAP uses to maintain public order, control inter-ethnic conflicts, and defend the state against subversives. It includes riot and crowd control, surveillance of suspect individuals and groups, undercover operations against special targets, the use of exceptional powers (e.g. detention without trial), and the paramilitary style of patrolling in the townships. Counter-insurgency policing is the dominant mode of policing in South Africa, firmly entrenched institutionally. The security of the state, not the safety of citizens, has always been the number-one priority, with ordinary crime, especially in the black townships, a secondary concern.

The SAP's infamous Security Branch of 4000 members has now been absorbed into a new Crime Combating and Investigation division (CCI), but many of its duties are the same as those of the old Security Branch (*Argus*, 24 May 1992) and it is headed by the same man, Lt-General Basie Smit. Riot squads, now called Internal Stability Units, have been expanded in the past three years. And police training continues to emphasise security and public order over ordinary police work.

The treatment of detainees remains a matter of grave concern. Reports of torture and other mistreatment have not ceased since 1990 and at least 29 people died in police custody during the 'reform' period of January 1990 through June 1992, many in suspicious circumstances (*South*, 1 August 1992). Recently, the country's leading pathologist, Dr Jonathan Gluckman, broke years of silence when he revealed that 90 per cent of the 200 deceased detainees on whom he had performed autopsies over the years had been murdered by the police and that such killings were continuing; he went public with the allegations only after failing in his private efforts to convince the President, the Police Commissioner, and the Minister of Law and Order of the problem (*New Nation*, 31 July 1992).

Public marches and gatherings are one of the most visible settings in which problems of counter-insurgency policing can be observed. While many gatherings pass without incident, the police have on several occasions grossly over-reacted with lethal force (Amnesty International, 1992). The ideal of minimum force is readily suspended when, as is often the case in South Africa, heavily-armed police are vastly outnumbered by protesters and when they are under lax control from superiors at the scene. The lack of command-and-control is a recurrent theme in situations that have gone awry. The Goldstone Commission (1990) found that the 1990 shootings of protesters in Sebokeng were a direct result of a 'general absence of coordination' and grossly undisciplined behaviour by police on the line facing the protesters. The commanding officer was sitting in his vehicle remote from his men when the shooting began and he gave no orders to shoot. The Commission called the shooting unjustified (the protesters posed no actual or imminent threat to the police) and indiscriminate (84 people were shot in the back as they were trying to flee), and it criticised the 'callous attitude' of the police who testified before it: 'They displayed an attitude of unconcern for the lethal nature of their ammunition and for the consequences of its use' (Goldstone Commission, 1990: p. 66).

Several of the Commission's recommendations were implemented, but serious problems remain. Two years on, another inquiry reached similar findings about the lack of discipline and supervision of police who fired on residents of Boipatong without an order to do so (Waddington Inquiry, 1992). And an international panel studying the larger problem of public-order policing found that police were too eager to use deadly force to disperse illegal but peaceful gatherings; the panel also questioned the use of special riot squads, the Internal Stability Units, recommending that well-trained local police be given primary responsibility for crowd-control situations (Heymann Panel, 1992).

Counter-insurgency policing SAP-style has serious consequences: not only is it conducive to human casualties, it also overshadows and detracts from reforms in policing, interferes with negotiations between the regime and opposition parties, and fuels intense national controversies and popular estrangement from the police and the state. This kind of policing has also diminished the SAP's capacity to fight crime. Serious crime reported to the police increased 8.5 per cent nationwide in 1990 and 9.8 per cent in 1991, and it is skyrocketing in the black townships (Commissioner of the South African Police, 1991, 1992). This crime wave requires urgent attention, in terms of both reactive and preventive measures, but it has not received the priority it deserves, in part because of the continuing commitment of resources to the counter-insurgency enterprise.

CONCLUSION

Dramatic improvement in the quality of policing and in the potential for the SAP to increase its popular legitimacy are contingent on – but not an automatic outgrowth of – the creation of a new political system that will break once and for all the link between the police and the apartheid state. As noted above, a new regime is a necessary, but not sufficient, condition for meaningful changes in police–community relations. Assuming that the new regime has an interest in and the will to press for police reform, its capacity to do so will be shaped by various factors, including the level of police resistance to change.

Having said that, a number of valuable changes can be made prior to the installation of a new regime – most importantly, in my view, in the area of counter-insurgency policing. In this vein, the SAP needs to abandon some security practices and take steps to blunt the abrasive manner in which it handles other problems. It is vital that the authorities put an end to the trigger-happy policing of protests and riots, surveillance of government opponents, the misuse of police powers on the street, undercover hit squads, and torture and murder of suspects in custody. The following specific reforms seem necessary:

• A system of lay visiting should be created to monitor conditions in police stations and prisons. Lay visitors should make frequent, unannounced visits to determine how detainees are being treated.

- The Police Board should give urgent attention to the process of demilitarising the SAP and to problems associated with security policing.
- As part of the overall demilitarisation of the SAP, the use of armoured Land Rovers (Casspirs) and other paramilitary vehicles should be discontinued in relatively peaceful townships. In more dangerous areas, this may not be feasible at present.
- Police who handle public order situations should act with greater restraint (using force incrementally), which requires that they be better trained, properly equipped, deployed in larger numbers, and governed by much stricter command and control.
- Officers attached to riot units for long periods (some for 10–12 years) should be retrained and transferred back to the regular force.
- The CCI's security police should be strictly confined to monitoring genuine threats to public order and state security, and they should cease their surveillance of the regime's political opponents.
- Officers who have committed illegal acts during counter-insurgency operations should be punished. Some police still believe they can literally get away with murder and it is imperative that severe sanctions be imposed by the SAP (e.g. dismissals) and by the criminal courts for any offence resulting in death or serious injury.

It is appreciated that, in a context of soaring criminal violence and political unrest, the SAP must retain its capacity to deal firmly with individual offenders and public-order problems. This context does not, however, preclude the changes outlined above.

Progressive reforms in the SAP's mission, training, composition and accountability are all several steps removed from the sharp edge of policing on the ground. What is urgently necessary is a liberalisation of security policing, coupled with visibly impartial law enforcement. These changes may pay dividends in terms of the public's experiences with and attitudes toward the SAP. But even if they do not have an immediate effect on popular perceptions, they are essential for the building of a modernised, professional police force.

REFERENCES

Africa Watch. 1991. *The Killings in South Africa: The Role of the Security Forces and the Response of the State* (New York).

Amnesty International. 1992. *South Africa: State of Fear* (New York).

Black Sash. 1988. *'Greenflies': Municipal Police in the Western Cape* (Cape Town, Black Sash).

Brewer, J. 1991a. *Inside the RVC: Routine Policing in a Divided Society* (Oxford, The Clarendon Press).

———. 1991b. 'Policing in Divided Societies', *Policing and Society* 1: 179–91.

———. 1994. *Black and Blue: Policing in South Africa* (Oxford, The Clarendon Press).

Centre for Criminal Justice. 1991. *Policing in the Greater Pietermaritzburg Area* (Pietermaritzburg, University of Natal).

CIIR [Catholic Institute for International Relations]. 1988. *Now Everyone is Afraid: The Changing Face of Policing in South Africa* (London, CIIR).

Commissioner of the South African Police. 1991. *Annual Report for 1990*.

———. 1992. *Annual Report for 1991*.

Fine, D. 1989. 'Kitskonstabels: A Case Study in Black-on-Black Policing', *Acta Juridica*: 44–85.

Foster, D. and C. Luyt. 1986. 'The Blue Man's Burden: Policing the Police in South Africa', *South African Journal on Human Rights* 2: 297–311.

Goldsmith, A. 1991. 'External Review and Self-Regulation', in A. Goldsmith (ed.), *Complaints Against the Police* (Oxford, The Clarendon Press).

Goldstone Commission. 1990. *Report of the Commission of Inquiry into the Incidents at Sebokeng, Boipatong, Lekoa, Sharpeville, and Evaton on 26 March 1990.* Johannesburg, 27 June.

Goldstone Commission. 1992. *Second Interim Report.* Commission on the Prevention of Public Violence and Intimidation, Cape Town, 29 April.

Grange, H. 1991. 'Police – Men in the Middle.' *Star*, 7 May.

Hansson, D. 1989. 'Trigger Happy? An Evaluation of Fatal Police Shootings in the Greater Cape Town Area', *Acta Juridica*: 118–38.

Haysom, N. 1990. 'Vigilantism and the Policing of African Townships', in D. Hansson and D. van Zyl Smit (eds), *Towards Justice? Crime and State Control in South Africa* (Cape Town, Oxford University Press).

Heymann Panel. 1992. *Testimony of Multinational Panel Regarding Lawful Control of Demonstrations in South Africa.* Presented to the Commission on the Prevention of Public Violence and Intimidation, Cape Town, 9 July.

Hofmeyr, B. and T. Shefer. 1987. *Bonguleto Report.* Institute of Criminology, University of Cape Town.

Human Rights Commission. 1992. *Checkmate for Apartheid* (Braamfontein, HRC).

International Commission of Jurists. 1992. Report of investigation reprinted in *Rights* 2 (July): 6–17.

Lansdown Commission. 1937. *Report of the Commission of Inquiry into Certain Matters Concerning the South African Police*. UG-50.

Ottaway, D. 1992. 'Adrift in S. Africa's "Beirut"'. *Washington Post*, 28 July.

Powell, I. 1991. 'Running Guns for Inkatha's Impis', *Star*, 28 July.

Powell, I. and E. Anderson. 1992. 'The SAP Blues: The Case Against the Security Forces', *Vrye Weekblad*, 26 June.

Reiner, R. 1985. *The Politics of the Police* (Brighton, Wheatsheaf).

Smith, T. 1992. 'Trust Feed Wasn't a One-Off Massacre', *Weekly Mail*, 15 May.

Stober, P. and G. Evans. 1991. 'A Random List of 23 Claims about "Blind-Eyed" Police', *Weekly Mail*, 2 August.

Waddington Inquiry. 1992. *Report of the Inquiry into the Police Response to, and Investigation of, Events in Boipatong on 17 June 1992*. Presented to the Commission on the Prevention of Public Violence and Intimidation, 20 July.

Walker, C. 1990. 'Police and Community in Northern Ireland', *Northern Ireland Legal Quarterly* 41: 105–42.

Weitzer, R. 1987a. 'Contested Order: The Struggle over British Security Policy in Northern Ireland', *Comparative Politics* 19: 281–98.

——. 1987b. 'Policing Northern Ireland Today', *Political Quarterly* 58: 88–96.

——. 1990. *Transforming Settler States: Communal Conflict and Internal Security in Northern Ireland and Zimbabwe* (Berkeley, University of California Press).

——. 1991. 'Elite Conflicts over Policing in South Africa: 1980–1990', *Policing and Society* 1: 257–68.

——. 1992. 'Northern Ireland's Police Liaison Committees', *Policing and Society* 2: 233–43.

Weitzer R. and C. Beattie. 1990. 'Police Killings in South Africa: Criminal Cases, 1984–1989'. Paper presented at the annual meeting of the American Society of Criminology, Baltimore.

5 Educational Desegregration

Anthony Lemon

INTRODUCTION

Since the Soweto revolt of 1976, and more especially since 1985 when a localised State of Emergency was first proclaimed and 'people's education' was conceived as an element in the liberation struggle, black education has been contested terrain in South African urban areas. Apartheid education has manifestly failed as an instrument of social control, a function which has yet to be restored. Today education is arguably 'the most important and intractable issue in South Africa's social fabric' (Lee *et al.*, 1991: p. 156). There is little chance that education can truly be depoliticised, because whatever the composition of a new government, its ability to meet people's expectations of improved life chances will be constrained by resource limitations. The educational strategy pursued will be of crucial importance to the peace and stability of a post-apartheid South Africa.

The focus of this chapter is primarily on resources, which operate as a fundamental constraint on the future transformation of educational opportunity for the poor. But we should recognise at the outset that the education crisis, while it is rooted in the inequalities of apartheid, has come to reflect concerns about the content, style, structures and objectives of school education. These are reflected in the brief history of the education struggle with which the chapter begins. Massive increases in the black education budget since the 1970s have done nothing to satisfy their recipients, and will not, as long as the state resists the central demand for a single education department administering a common school system for all South Africans. It now concedes the inevitability of such a development,[1] but argues that it must await the (negotiated) replacement of the 1984 constitution. This leads to the paradox of a government which in 1991 repealed the Population Registration Act and thereby

91

deprived itself of the ability to classify people by race, but which retains an educational system wholly dependent on such classification.

The National Party government is using the time it has to introduce reforms, especially in the white education sector. It will be argued that in moving to a degree of privatisation, the government is seeking to protect whites from the otherwise inevitable consequences of desegregation and redistribution. Such policies are likely to contribute, together with the private sector *per se*, to the gradual replacement of racial divisions with class divisions. But even within the state sector there remain major geographical constraints on the redistribution of resources which relate, *inter alia*, to demography, the location of educational infrastructure and problems of teacher redeployment. Particular attention is given to huge but relatively neglected urban/rural disparities which, it is argued, should be at the forefront of future redistributive strategies. If these disparities are to be addressed, finite resources must limit what the state can afford to provide as a universal right. Beyond such provision, socio-economic differences are bound to influence educational opportunity, and strategies to minimise disadvantage will need to be considered.

INHERITED STRUCTURES, LIBERATION STRUGGLE AND STATE RESPONSES

The inequalities inherent in apartheid education are well known. During the 1950s and 1960s black educational expenditure was tied to black taxes, creating a negative-feedback situation. Black pupils and teachers were also forced to use an overtly biased and racist syllabus. It was an educational issue – a new insistence that mathematics and social science be taught and examined in Afrikaans – which sparked the Soweto revolt in 1976, and thus marked the beginning of a fierce and unresolved struggle. The state implicitly recognised the need for major policy changes, but its responses, in the de Lange Report (HSRC, 1981) and the 1983 White Paper (South Africa, 1983) remained 'firmly locked within a segregationist framework' (Nasson 1990a: p. 58). Since the introduction of the 1984 constitution, education has been largely deemed the 'own affair' of each population group, with separate education ministries for whites, coloured people, Indians, and for each of the ten homelands or bantustans (including the four nominally independent states). The exception was black education in non-homeland areas, which was anomalously deemed a 'general affair' under its own national education department, headed by whites.

Black protest against such educational structures intensified in the mid-1980s. It was linked to wider community and political issues, reflected in the slogan 'Liberation now – education later' (Unterhalter and Wolpe, 1991). The state reacted repressively, banning COSAS in 1985 and virtually banning the National Education Crisis Committee (NECC) during the State of Emergency in the years 1986–90. In December 1989 the latter sought to restructure itself as a broader coordinating committee, changing its name accordingly. It launched a back-to-school campaign which was powerfully supported by Nelson Mandela soon after his release from prison in February 1990. His message underlined the dichotomy inherent in black attitudes to education, which is seen both as a gateway and a barrier: 'an emotional ambiguity, deep and pervasive, that has to be added to the normal clash of interests involved in policy system change in other countries' (Lee *et al.*, 1991: p. 151).

CONCESSION AND COMPROMISE: STATE POLICIES, 1990–92

The state's educational policies have done little to assuage this ambiguity since the lifting of restrictions and the unbanning of the ANC and other groups in February 1990. In mid-1992 education accounted for most of the laws remaining on the statute book which still embody discrimination in terms of race. There was no real liberalisation, let alone the democratisation demanded by the NECC and other groups (which is not without problems in the education sphere). Instead education was still very obviously in a phase of concession and compromise, giving ground slowly in response to changing perceptions of its own interests as well as interest-group pressures. Nowhere is this better reflected than in the twists and turns of its policy towards admissions and the financing and management of white schools. As these have emerged during 1992, however, they have begun to develop a longer-term significance, both in terms of what the government is seeking to save for whites, and as pointers to the socially divisive consequences of resource limitations for a post-apartheid government.

In the late 1980s, rigid state-school segregation led to an increasing surplus of school places for whites. Despite the closure of 203 schools between 1981 and 1991, the number of unfilled places increased from 153 637 in 1986 to 287 387 in 1991 (Metcalfe, 1991: pp.13–14). These unfilled places resulted in part from a decline in the white birth rate, but also from changing demographic patterns in inner-city and some suburban areas, including the 'greying' of certain white residential areas in the closing years of the Group Areas Act. White schools in such areas were threatened with closure while parents of other race groups were forced to bus their children to schools for their own race group, even when racial mixing become legal in some of these areas under the Free Settlement Areas Act of 1988. In the areas most affected, such anomalies led to some white parental and school authority pressure to allow white state schools to admit pupils of other races.

Whereas the state's first reaction to black pressures has usually been repressive, white pressures required a more positive response. This came in the introduction of three new school models in September 1990: parents could opt to go private, with a 45 per cent subsidy (model A), state-aided, with the state paying staff salaries (model C), or to manage their own admissions policy, subject to conditions intended to preserve their cultural character, but remain fully state-financed (model B). Schools wishing to change status were required to hold an official poll of parents; an 80 per cent turnout was required, and 72 per cent of those entitled to vote had to support the change. Even then ministerial consent depended on a number of other considerations (South Africa, 1990). Given the sensitivity of the issue for most whites, it was widely assumed that such conditions would discourage adoption of the models in all but a handful of schools. The new policy clearly represented a deeply cautious, controlled approach to desegregation.

The results were unexpected. Just over 10 per cent of all white schools voted to change at the earliest opportunity, and a second round of ballots had increased this figure to 23 per cent by August 1991, when a further 9 per cent of schools were waiting to vote and many requests to do so were still being received. The distribution of schools opting to change was overwhelmingly urban. In Natal, 67.7 per cent of schools voting for change were in Durban and Pietermaritzburg. Johannesburg alone counted for 56.2 per cent of Transvaal schools voting for change; with Pretoria and the East Rand the percentage rose to 81. Metropolitan predominance was rather less evident in the Cape Province, where desegregation was most widely accepted: Cape Town and the Cape Peninsula accounted for just half the schools voting for change, and the neighbouring Stellenbosch and Boland areas for a further 10.5 per cent; but other cities (East London 11.9 per cent, Port Elizabeth 7.7 per cent) and smaller, mainly English-speaking Eastern Cape towns of Grahamstown, Queenstown, and King William's Town also helped to lead the way. In the northern Cape and the Orange Free State, change was virtually confined to Kimberley and Bloemfontein, and affected only a dozen schools in these predominantly Afrikaans-speaking cities.

As the above distribution implies, change was largely confined to English-medium schools: by August 1991 no less than 95 per cent of these had voted for change in the Cape province, 79 per cent in Natal and 38 per cent in the Transvaal. By mid-1992, however, an increasing number of Afrikaans-medium schools were requesting ballots.

Official policy moved to some extent with the tide of white opinion. Ministerial permission soon became automatic when the ballot requirements were satisfied, and was granted in many 'near-miss' cases too. In what amounted to a minor U-turn, a new model D was announced in August 1991, which would allow white schools with seriously decreasing enrolments to be transferred to black education departments, or transformed into open schools under the control of the (white) Department of Education and Culture (DEC).

The unexpectedly positive response to model B extended well beyond schools threatened with closure, while the latter factor had not noticeably weakened Afrikaner parents' attachment to segregation. In the rapidly changing political climate prevailing since February 1990, English-speaking parents, at least, appear to have accepted the inevitability of desegregated schools. Some

undoubtedly welcomed it, but more probably embraced change
for conservative reasons, believing that control over their own
admissions policies could enable more measured change than
might ultimately be forced on other state schools. Certainly the
admissions policies adopted suggest schools anxious to protect
their academic standards and, in the words of Bryanston High
School, Johannesburg, their 'culture ecology'.[2] By January 1991,
when the first round of admissions to model B schools was
completed, only 6059 blacks had been admitted to 'open'
schools – an average of only 30 per school (Bot, 1991a: p. 4).

Schools chose overwhelmingly to vote on model B: model A
was totally ignored, and less than fifty schools, mainly in the
Transvaal, opted for model C. This clearly suggests that, whatever the perceived advantages of controlling their own admissions policies, few schools or parents wished to pay for the
privilege, even in affluent suburbs. In February 1992, however,
official policy changed again, driven this time, it appeared, by
budgetary constraints in a time of continuing economic recession. New staffing provision scales were introduced for the
(white) DEC which implied the retrenchment of 11 000 teachers.
A related budget-cut of 17 per cent followed. Ostensibly to
minimise teacher retrenchment, the government proposed that
all DEC schools should adopt model C in August 1992, unless
two-thirds of parents voted against it, in which case they could
retain the *status quo*, but with fewer teachers and reduced
funding. Ownership of buildings and grounds, furniture and
equipment would be transferred free of charge to model C
schools. They would then become responsible for maintenance,
which accounted for an estimated 17 per cent of total costs. Fee
payment would become compulsory: initial estimates suggested
that the cost would be about three times the amount of the
voluntary levies made hitherto, but both the size of the latter
and the predicted fee levels varied widely.

The threat of reduced teaching and maintenance provision
put heavy pressure on parents to accept the change, while the
two-thirds requirement increased the difficulty of rejection,
especially given the limited time available to organise a ballot
and influence opinion. So in May the DEC was able to announce
that 95.8 per cent of its schools had 'accepted' model C.

Within eighteen months the government had moved from
insistence on ballot requirements clearly intended to minimise

adoption of the new models to the virtual imposition of one of them. At one level this may be viewed as evidence of its uncertainty in a period of rapid transition. But the shift to model C has more profound implications in terms of both the government's long-term aims and the probable consequences of redistribution by a future government.

Reduction of the DEC budget was consistent both with the government's proclaimed strategy of equalising per capita education (see below), and the undoubted constraints of the overall economic situation. The DEC's response was condemned by the Democratic Party's education spokesman as 'a frightening disposal of family silver for a short-term budgetary expedient',[3] but it was arguably much more than this. Most schools could have survived the 1992 cuts in their generous teacher:pupil ratios without disaster, but if cuts of this magnitude emanated from a white government, the single education department of a majority government might be expected to wield the axe far more ruthlessly. The only way to resist the logical implications of equal per capita resourcing was a rapid move to semi-privatisation, and one which, given the previous evidence of voting on models A, B and C, would have to be effectively imposed on parents who had, for the most part, not begun to realise the resource implications of equal per capita education spending.

By transferring assets to the schools themselves, the government undoubtedly intends to make reversal of these changes more difficult for its successor. Small wonder that the South African Democratic Teachers Union believed that the budget was being used as a smokescreen to restructure white education before a democratic solution to the entire education crisis could be found through the process of negotiation.[4] The semi-privatisation of DEC schools will effectively take them out of reach of all but middle-class blacks. Class will gradually replace race as the distinguishing feature of model C schools, as it has already in much of the private sector proper. In the post-apartheid period, it is not difficult to see a class alliance arising in defence of these schools – an alliance based, appropriately enough, on the property rights which the present government will fight hard to enshrine in a new constitution.

There are implications here for the whole redistributive strategy of a post-apartheid government. The determination of whites (and increasingly of a wider middleclass) to maintain high standards of education provision will not disappear with the advent of a new political dispensation. They will undoubtedly find ways of doing so, inside or outside the state system. If the compromise of model C were to disappear, the return of voluntary levies, at a much higher level than in the 1980s, seems virtually certain unless it becomes illegal. In this event, a major growth of the private sector can be envisaged.

The example of Zimbabwe is instructive here. Since 1982 parents in some government schools have used management status agreements between the Ministry of Education and parent associations to avoid the full consequences of the substantial erosion in public expenditure per pupil. But the government has not provided full legal or political support for this status (Reynolds, 1990: p. 146), and many middle-class parents, including most whites, have transferred their children to the private sector. Reynolds proposes an ingenious if somewhat complex way of overcoming this duality in what he believes to be a socially acceptable way. Management status agreements, and the associated levies on parents, would receive full official support, but the levies would be taxed for the benefit of schools in poorer areas; the deterrent effect of the tax would in turn be mitigated by incentives to schools based on their performance in collecting levies (Reynolds, 1990: pp. 148–52). The advantage of such a system is clear: the middle classes could be induced to stay within the national education system, and parents could contribute their resources, management and other skills to the benefit of all within the state system.

This critique of late-apartheid policies has taken for granted overall resource constraints. It is now time to scrutinise these more closely, first in national terms, and then with reference to specific constraints.

EXISTING INEQUALITIES AND RESOURCE IMPLICATIONS

South Africa's notorious disparities in racial per capita spending have been gradually reduced, but remain substantial. The black share of the overall education budget, including the ten homelands, doubled from 24 per cent in 1979/80 to 48 per cent in

1991/2 (SAIRR, 1992: p.193). In April 1986 a ten-year plan to move towards parity of per capita expenditure was announced. The following year the Minister of National Education said that the government had committed itself to a real increase in educational expenditure of 4.1 per cent a year for the next ten years, and had drafted formulae designed to bring about parity, but this would not necessarily be fully achieved within the period of the plan (SAIRR, 1988: p. 150). Political and economic realities forced the government to announce in April 1989 that the plan could not be implemented (SAIRR, 1990: p.788), but per capita spending on black education continued to increase from 20 per cent of the white figure in 1985/6 to 25 per cent in 1989/90;[5] the corresponding figures for coloured people and Indians were 53 per cent and 71 per cent respectively (SAIRR, 1992: p. 195).

The implications of such inequalities are revealed by a multitude of data on enrolment, teacher:pupil ratios (TPRs) and teacher qualifications. TPRs in non-homeland areas in 1991 were 39:1 for Africans, 24:1 for coloured people, 18:1 for Indians and 17:1 for whites (DBSA, 1992). Classroom:pupil ratios for blacks were substantially worse than TPRs. The proportion of school pupils receiving secondary education in 1988 was 23.7 per cent for blacks and 27.4 per cent for coloured people, but 39.6 per cent for Indians and 42.8 per cent for whites. Contrasts in the proportion reaching standard 10 (the final year) are much greater: only 2.7 per cent of blacks and coloured people, compared with 5.7 per cent of Indians and 7.7 per cent of whites (SAIRR, 1990: pp. 824–5). Dropout rates for blacks are such that of 10 000 blacks who start school, only 113 pass matriculation (leaving) examinations.[6]

The poor qualifications of many black teachers constitute another major problem. In 1990 only 53 per cent of secondary teachers in DET schools met the official minimum requirement of standard 10 plus three years of teacher training, although this had improved from 42 per cent two years earlier; the equivalent figure for the self-governing homelands was 50 per cent (SAIRR, 1992: p. 209). In primary schools 15 per cent lacked even the minimum qualification of standard 6 and a diploma, a figure rising to 22 per cent in the six self-governing homelands.

Recent black matriculation rates demonstrate the effects of disruption in township schools (Table 5.1), in terms of both the low overall black pass-rates and the marked geographical

Table 5.1   Matriculation results

(i) results by race group, 1988–90 (% pass rate)

Year	Black	Coloured	Indian	White
1988	40.7	66.1	95.1	96.1
1989	40.9	72.7	93.6	96.0
1990	37.0	79.4	95.0	95.9

(ii) Black results by region and homeland, 1990 (% pass)

DET schools	*1990*	*Self-governing homelands*	*1990*
Cape	34	Gazankulu	36
Diamond Fields	35	KaNgwane	38
Highveld	31	KwaNdebele	29
Johannesburg	26	KwaZulu	43
Natal	41	Lebowa	28
Northern Transvaal	44	QwaQwa	31
		'Independent' homelands	
OFS	28	Bophuthatswana	52
Orange–Vaal	38	Ciskei	43
		Transkei	44
		Venda	40

Sources: SAIRR 1990, pp. 829–31 and 1992, p. 208;
            Star (Johannesburg), 14 May 1991.

variations which occurred. In 1990 the disastrous results in troubled Witwatersrand schools stand out, whereas in Natal and the northern Transvaal, regions where fewer teachers participated in strikes and sit-ins, results were well above the national average, as they were in KwaZulu and the four 'independent' homelands. The 1990 pass rates improved somewhat after supplementary examinations in March 1991, reaching 40.7 per cent.[7]

Overall resource constraints are best captured by the fact that in 1991–92, 21 per cent of budgetary expenditure, a figure equal to 6.2 per cent of GDP, was allocated to education. No government is likely to increase these figures significantly. Improvements in state education for blacks are thus dependent on redistribution within the global education budget, and/or on renewed economic growth. No one seriously believes that current white per capita spending levels can be extended to the whole population: 1992 estimates by Senbank and the University of Pretoria suggest that this would consume 42 per cent of budgetary expenditure and 11 per cent of GDP (SAIRR, 1992: pp. 196 and 226).[8]

In June 1991 the government committee investigating an education renewal strategy (ERS) published a wide-ranging discussion document (South Africa, 1991). Like the de Lange Report a decade earlier, it treated education as an essentially technical problem (Nasson, 1990a) paying little overt attention to political demands or the redressing of historical imbalances. It was not specific in terms of financial provision or means of implementation (Christie, 1991). Nevertheless, most of its recommendations are at least feeling the way towards a unified, non-racial and more decentralised education system, and show awareness of resource constraints. Many of its recommendations are similar to those of de Lange, but in so far as this document was formulated by the education departments of government instead of an outside body, it does reflect a departure in official thinking (Bot, 1991b).

From a resource standpoint, the document's key proposal for school education is that state expenditure should be linked primarily to a minimum period of compulsory education, including one year's compulsory pre-primary education to help deprived children bridge the gap to school, and the current seven years of primary school; this should be extended as circumstances permit. At present there is no compulsory education for blacks, except at schools where parents request this, whereas secondary education is compulsory for whites and coloured people (to the age of 16 or until they have passed standard 8) and Indians (to the age of 15). 'Exit points' from the formal education system are identified at standards 5 (the end of primary education), 7 and 10 (matriculation), leading to further structured education in the non-formal sector – vocational training on the job leading to certification. In the senior secondary phase (standards 8–10), subject packages could be constructed with an emphasis on either general (i.e. more academic) or more vocationally-orientated education.

Management councils would be established at all schools, with greater autonomy but also with responsibility for finance to supplement state provision. Building standards would be scaled down. Most importantly, in secondary schools, the assumption of the ERS document is that costs would be borne mainly by parents and by the private sector.

Such a strategy would by no means guarantee equality of opportunity in practice. The financial responsibility of management councils would effectively convert all South African schools to the equivalent of model C schools, and lead to wide variation in overall levels of provision according to the financial capacity of each community. The constraints responsible for such a proposal are indisputable, but it could perhaps benefit from attention to Reynolds's (1990) Zimbabwean proposals, discussed above. Those leaving the formal system at the earlier points proposed would almost certainly be overwhelmingly children of poor families, rather than those more suited to this channel. Within the secondary schools themselves, a similar danger exists that the choice between general and vocational subjects would frequently be made more in terms of socio-economic background than aptitude.

Criticism of the ERS document or any other education strategy is all too easy in the context of inherited inequalities and the highly-politicised nature of the education debate. All strategies must, however, include a plan for funding education fairly and with maximum effectiveness within the resources available: in the words of F. W. de Klerk himself, when Minister of National Education, 'we shall have to provide better education with fewer resources per client by means of a more efficient and leaner system of education'.[9] The final section of this chapter gives more detailed attention to some of the less-publicised constraints which will act upon the adoption and implementation of an educational strategy by a post-apartheid government.

OTHER CONSTRAINTS ON REDISTRIBUTION

Demography is the greatest constraint on the potential for redistribution in South Africa's education system. Population ratios alone suggest that redistribution from the privileged sector will be thinly spread, and this holds true even if (as seems inevitable) Indians and coloured people end up on the 'losing side' of a non-racial system: the three groups combined account for only just over a quarter of the total population. Redistribution will also have to take into account those blacks of school age who are not in school: estimates vary from 1.5 to 6 million.[10] This is at the end of a decade in which black pupil enrolment has increased from 4.8 million in 1980 to 6.8 million in 1990: already blacks represent 79 per cent of total enrolment, and one black person in four is at school (SAIRR, 1992: p. 183). The Research Institute for Education Planning at the University of the Orange Free State has estimated that the number of black pupils will rise to 9.3 million by 1995 and 13.9 million, or 84 per cent of all school pupils, by the year 2000.[11]

Expansion of this order will severely limit growth in per capita spending. It also poses major problems of teacher supply, especially of qualified teachers. To some extent these can be eased by a more equitable distribution of teachers within a unified education system. This implies equalisation of TPRs at a much less generous level than that now existing for whites, Indians and coloured people. The World Bank (1988) argues that changes of class-size within the range 25 to 50 pupils have very little effect on performance. Using this evidence, Moulder (1991) shows that use of a TPR of 1:35 to allocate the teachers in all departments in 1987 would actually produce a surplus of teachers; a TPR of 1:40 would increase the surplus to 44 764.

A unified education department would end the absurdity of retrenching teachers in the employ of the (white) Department of Education and Culture when they are badly needed elsewhere. However, there must be serious doubt that many serving teachers would be prepared to move to black schools, or indeed to remote rural schools, as an efficient deployment of resources will certainly demand. For married women, who comprise an important part of the teaching force, such moves may be impossible, while the image of township schools will prove a major deterrent to most whites. Even in predominantly white schools, the doubling of class-sizes implied by Moulder's TPRs would undoubtedly lead to some resignations by teachers used to a gentler professional existence. This in no way questions the logic of equalising TPRs, but it does mean that this will not in itself wholly resolve the quantitative aspects of teacher supply, let alone the qualitative problem, which could worsen in the short term with the loss of qualified white teachers.

If people can be immobile, school plant is unavoidably so. The repeal of the Group Areas Act in 1991 was essentially a passive measure, in the sense that the apartheid cities which were so ruthlessly forged will not be eradicated for decades to come (Lemon, 1991). The best school buildings and grounds will remain where they are now, in suburbs likely to remain predominantly white, while many black secondary schools will remain without science laboratories for a long time. Equal expenditure will shift the burden of maintenance to parents in the affluent suburbs (as model C has already begun to do), but it will not lessen existing infrastructural inequality: this would require positive discrimination.

Apartheid has naturally focused attention on racial inequalities, but differences between urban and rural provision are also profound.[12] Nasson (1990a: p. 76) condemned the de Lange strategy as 'servicing the needs of metropolitan growth zones', while Buckland (1982: p. 25) commented that the rural population 'seems to feature only as a problem'. For purposes of analysis, rural areas must be divided into homelands and areas under DET control, which are essentially white commercial farming areas. Blacks in the latter generally receive the worst educational provision of any group in South Africa. They are dependent on farm schools which are opened (and closed) by farmers themselves, and many newspaper reports bear testimony to their precarious existence. In 1988 a mere 1.43 per cent of the half-million pupils at farm schools were receiving secondary education. Large areas of the country, such as the Border region and northern part of the eastern Cape, have no secondary facilities at all for blacks.[13] The government subsidises transport to urban schools for white, coloured and Indian children living on farms, but not for blacks, who must often walk long distances even to the nearest farm schools.

In 1988 the DET announced that it was increasing its contribution to physical facilities from 50 to 75 per cent; farmowners in certain border areas have received subsidies of 75–80 per cent (SAIRR, 1992: p. 202) as part of the state's policy of supporting farms in these regions for strategic reasons. The

DET pays the salaries of teachers, many of whom are unqualified, and has instituted a programme of management training for all farm-school teachers. But in the 1988–89 financial year, the average DET subsidy per pupil in farm schools was R261 per year (SAIRR, 1990: p. 820), barely one-third of the average in all DET schools, and less than one-tenth of white per capita spending.

The position in the homelands varies considerably. They are, of course, by no means wholly rural, and include huge functionally urban areas of informal settlement within commuting distance of cities such as Durban, East London and Pretoria, which are growing so fast that school provision lags far behind. The particularly rapid growth of the greater Durban thus contributes to exceptionally high 1990 TPRs of 1:53 (primary) and 1:42 (secondary) in KwaZulu. The most favourable TPRs are 1:32 (primary) in QwaQwa and 1:32 (secondary) in Bophuthatswana (SAIRR, 1992: pp. 205–6). In the six self-governing homelands, 22 per cent of primary school teachers and 10 per cent of secondary teachers were unqualified in 1990, compared with 15 per cent and 3 per cent respectively in DET schools (SAIRR, 1992: p. 209).

The greatest inequalities, however, are in terms of buildings and equipment. When salaries are deducted from per capita expenditure, little remains in many of the homelands. Science laboratories are almost non-existent. Desperate classroom shortages are reflected in 1988 primary classroom:pupil ratios of 1:88 (Transkei), 1:77 (Gazankulu) and 1:76 (KaNgwane), and secondary school ratios of 1:66 (Lebowa) and 1:62 (KaNgwane). Figures for DET schools in 1988 were 1:42 (primary) and 1:46 (secondary). Other homelands are better-off, notably Bophuthatswana, QwaQwa and, for secondary classrooms, Transkei (SAIRR, 1990: pp. 826–7).

The situation in both farm and homeland schools is considerably worse than these figures suggest, because they exclude children who are not at school at all (see above), the majority of whom are in rural areas. If the rural/urban differences in funding and infrastructure are to be closed, then Moulder (1991) is probably correct in arguing that black urban education is as well-funded now as it is going to be. In other words, resource constraints are likely to dictate average per capita spending in all state schools in a unified education system no greater than current levels of DET spending in the townships. Given that these townships are the very places where the educational struggle has been strongest and most politicised, and their schools the ones which have attracted international media attention to educational inequality in South Africa, this is indeed a sobering thought. Yet the need to ensure that 'rural Africans will not be ignored or short-changed when power and wealth are fundamentally redistributed in a transformed society' (Beinart and Bundy, 1987: p. ix) is as pressing as the removal of racial discrimination from the education system.

Finally, mention must be made of a less geographical aspect of inequality, albeit one where rural areas again fare worst. This concerns the very low numbers of black pupils taking mathematics and science, technical and even commercial subjects. In 1989, a mere 0.4 per cent took technical courses. In the 1990 examinations, 35 per cent of black candidates wrote mathematics, but a mere 6 per cent passed, compared with a 58 per cent white pass rate. Of 23 per cent writing physical science, 7 per cent passed, compared with 41 per cent of whites (SAIRR, 1992: p. 188). DET sources have recently been quoted as admitting that only 1 in 200 black schoolchildren matriculates with a standard of mathematics adequate for study at university and technikons.[14] Such statistics are the context of a comment in a leaked Chamber of Mines memorandum that 'all the efforts of the DET are immaterial to the mining industry'.[15] Reformist efforts designed to meet changing capitalist labour needs are only beginning to overcome the inheritance of Bantu Education.

CONCLUSION

Three major points are worth emphasising in conclusion: they concern what remains of the 'late apartheid' transition, the critical role of resources for a post-apartheid government, and the limits of education itself as a redistributive process.

We have seen that current reforms and policy proposals tend towards the replacement of racial with class divisions. While recognising the long-term difficulty of avoiding some element of this prescription, the present government positively seeks it, whereas its successor must strive to minimise it. Current reforms, and especially attempts to reduce racial disparities in education expenditure, are welcome in themselves, but they emanate from a government in whose election blacks paid no part, and they continue to be implemented in terms of the apartheid education structures decreed by the present constitution. Until the establishment of an interim government and the introduction of a unified education system, pressure can only continue to be directed, as Neville Alexander (1990: pp. 166–7) puts its, at 'finding, creating and exploiting spaces within the system' and so altering 'both the dynamic and the direction of the totality that confronts us'.

Some of these spaces are being filled by a multitude of different actors outside the public sector. Collectively, the private sector is responsible for a confusing and rapidly growing number of educational initiatives and projects: coordination is difficult if not impossible. While all this energy can only add up to tinkering with the present system, it does give the private sector some leverage to pressure the present government to move from its own tinkering to the beginnings of a longer-term strategy, however flawed, which is reflected in the ERS discussion document.

Both overall and specific resource constraints have emerged all too clearly in this chapter. It is vital for future political stability that these are more widely appreciated and understood: as Nattrass (1989: p. 181) has observed, 'glossing over substantial competing claims for scarce resources with slippery political promises, simply propels the problem into the future when it will come home to roost with a vengeance'. Equity demands not only the equalising of per capita expenditure, but the concentration of resources for buildings and equipment on deprived areas for an indefinite period. Nothing less than transformation is required. Renewed and sustained growth in the national economy will be absolutely critical if such redistribution is to mean any real improvement for the children of the poor. Without such an improvement, not only will individuals continue to be denied opportunity, but human potential will continue to be wasted and the economy will continue to suffer critical shortages of skilled and professional/managerial labour.

Finally, it is necessary to sound a note of caution. In a review of the international literature, Nasson (1990b) has assembled abundant evidence that faith in the independent capacity of expanded schooling to redistribute income is misplaced. Even transformation of educational opportunity will not of itself bring higher status and earnings to more than a fraction of the urban poor, and an even smaller fragment of the rural poor (Nasson, 1990b: p. 97). Education *per se* will do little to undermine the recognised inequalities of any capitalist society. Yet economic growth is essential to generate employment opportunities for those who have taken advantage of new educational opportunities. It will be the unenviable task of a post-apartheid government to judge how far it can afford to modify the distribution of wealth created by capitalism without jeopardising the growth on which both educational and employment opportunity depend.

NOTES

1. In May 1991 the Minister of National Education pleaded with opposition groups that a single education system was 'absolutely in the pipeline', and that it was no longer necessary to fight for it (*Citizen*, Pretoria, 14 May 1991).
2. *Business Day* (Johannesburg), 17 June 1991.
3. *Citizen*, 18 June 1992.
4. *Citizen*, 19 February 1992.
5. In 1990–91 this figure reached 26.8 per cent, according to a report in *Business Day* (Johannesburg), 6 February 1991.
6. Data from Research Institute for Education Planning, Bloemfontein, cited in *Productivity South Africa* 16 (4), August/September 1990.
7. *Star* (Johannesburg), 14 May 1991.
8. Even these figures reflect the considerable closure of the racial spending gap which has already been achieved. Nattrass (1989), working on educational expenditures in Natal–KwaZulu for 1983–84, calculated that to bring everyone of school age (including those not currently in school) up to white per capita spending levels would cost the equivalent of 123 per cent of the combined spending of all state departments in Natal and KwaZulu.
9. *Business Day*, 15 March 1990.
10. Estimates include 1.5 million (James Moulder, quoted in the *Star*, 27 February 1991); 3.5–5 million (Christian Research, Education and Information for Democracy, reported in the *Citizen*, 5 June 1991); and the Southern Africa Catholic Bishops Conference estimated the figure to be 6 million (*Business Day*, 25 June 1991).

11. *Education and Manpower Development* 10, 1989; cited in SAIRR 1992, p. 204.
12. Professor James Moulder of the Department of Philosophy at the University of Natal, Pietermaritzburg, has been almost a lone voice drawing attention to the rural/urban divide. See SAIRR 1990, p. 797 and 1992, p. 194, and the *Star*, 10 January 1991. Dr Neil McGurk, a prominent Roman Catholic headmaster and educationist, has also drawn attention to this issue (*Star*, 6 May 1991).
13. *Daily Dispatch* (East London), 25 June 1991.
14. *Sunday Times* (Johannesburg), 17 March 1991.
15. Ibid.

REFERENCES

Note: SAIRR = South African Institute of Race Relations
DBSA = Development Bank of Southern Africa

Alexander, N. 1990. 'Educational Strategies for a New South Africa', in B. Nasson and J. Samuel (eds), op. cit.
Beinart, W. and Bundy, C. 1987. *Hidden Struggles in Rural South Africa: Politics and Popular Movements in the Transkei and Eastern Cape, 1890–1930* (Johannesburg, Ravan).
Bot, M. 1991a. 'Open White Schools – Event or Non-event?', *South Africa Foundation News* 17 (3): 4.
——. 1991b. *Social and Economic Update 15: Special Issue on Education Renewal* (Johannesburg, SAIRR).
Buckland, P. 1982. 'The Education Crisis in South Africa: Restructuring the Policy Discourse', *Social Dynamics* 8 (1): 14–28.
Christie, P. 1991. Quoted in *The Star*, 3 July, and personal communication.
DBSA. 1992. *Education in South Africa, A Regional Overview; 1991* (Halfway House, DBSA).
HSRC (Human Sciences Research Council). 1981. *Education Provision in the RSA* (De Lange Report; Pretoria, Government Printer).
Lemon, A. (ed.).1991. *Homes Apart: South Africa's Segregated Cities* (London, Paul Chapman).
Lee, R., Schlemmer, L., Stack, L., Van Antwerpen, J. and Van Dyk, H. 1991. 'Policy Change and the Social Fabric' in R. Lee and L. Schlemmer (eds). *Transition to Democracy: Policy Perspectives* (Cape Town, Oxford University Press).
Metcalfe, M. 1991. *Desegregating Education in South Africa: White School Enrolments in Johannesburg, 1985–1991: Update and Policy Analysis*, Research Report No. 2, Education Policy Unit, University of the Witwatersrand, Johannesburg.
Moulder, J. 1991. 'Unequal Inequalities: Teacher:Pupil Ratios', *Indicator SA* 8(2): 76–8.

Nasson, B. 1990a. 'Redefining Inequality: Education Reform and the State in Contemporary South Africa', in B. Nasson and J. Samuel (eds), op. cit.

Nasson, B. 1990b. 'Education and Poverty', in B. Nasson and J. Samuel (eds), op. cit.

Nasson, B. and Samuel, J. (eds). 1990. *Education: From Poverty to Liberty* (Cape Town and Johannesburg, David Philip).

Nattrass, N. 1989. 'The KwaNatal Indaba and the Politics of Promising Too Much', in J. Brewer (ed.), *Can South Africa Survive?* (London, Macmillan).

Robinson, P. 1982. 'Where Stands an Educational Policy Towards the Poor?', *Educational Review* 34 (1): 27–33.

SAIRR. 1988. *Race Relations Survey 1987/8* (Johannesburg, SAIRR).

SAIRR. 1990. *Race Relations Survey 1989/90* (Johannesburg, SAIRR).

SAIRR. 1992. *Race Relations Survey 1991/92* (Johannesburg, SAIRR).

South Africa. 1983. *White Paper on the Provision of Education in the RSA* (Pretoria, Government Printer).

South Africa. 1990. *Additional Models for the Provision of Schooling: Information Document* (House of Assembly: Department of Education and Culture, Administration).

South Africa. 1991. *Education Renewal Strategy, Discussion Document* (Pretoria, Committee of Heads of Education Departments, Department of National Education).

Unterhalter, E. and Wolpe, H. 1991. 'Reproduction, Reform and Trans-formation: The Analysis of Education in South Africa', in E. Unterhalter, H. Wolpe, T. Botha, S. Badat, T. Dlamini and B. Khotseng (eds). *Apartheid Education and Popular Struggles in South Africa* (Johannesburg, Ravan).

World Bank. 1988. *Education in Sub-Saharan Africa: Policies for Adjustment, Revitalization and Expansion* (Washington DC, World Bank).

6 Constitutional Reform: The Absence of an Inclusive Middleground

Kierin O'Malley

INTRODUCTION

This chapter provides an analysis of the process of negotiated transition away from apartheid. After highlighting the most important developments in the process of negotiated transition between February 1990 and June 1992, the chapter assesses the degree to which the major contending regime models that existed at the beginning of the process of negotiated transition have moved toward one another. A central argument of the analysis is that the lack of agreement among the major parties on the essential nature of South African society, prompts a pessimistic view of the constitution-making process and its likelihood of achieving agreement, and thus future peace and stability. Contrary to a widely-held view, the process of negotiated transition has operated largely within a normative vacuum – a fact highlighted by the dominance of procedural over substantive issues. An inclusive political middleground remains elusive. The absence of the requisite degree of fundamental societal consensus bodes ill for the future.

POLITICAL TRANSITION IN SOUTH AFRICA IN THE 1990s: NEGOTIATIONS

South Africa's latest attempt at political transition away from the era of apartheid has been in progress since 1990. Negotiations as a mode of political transition in South Africa were preceded by three other ultimately unsuccessful attempts at terminating white domination. The multi-faceted, often incoherent and hesitant reform initiatives undertaken by the National Party government in the 1970s and the first half of the

111

1980s thus form part of a broader, overall process of transition away from apartheid in South Africa. Thus, the present period of negotiated transition was preceded by failed periods of government-initiated reform and ANC revolt, which have left legacies which seriously complicate the creation of an inclusive democratic society (Slabbert, 1992: p. 29).

Four ideal-typical modes of transition away from authoritarianism have been identified – imposition, revolution, reform and pacting (Slabbert, 1992: p. 6). Reform and pacting result from multilateral compromise as opposed to unilateral imposition, but differ in that, while reform involves mass pressure from below, pacting involves agreements at leadership-elite level (Slabbert 1992: pp. 6–7). Like much of the literature on transitions from authoritarian forms of government elsewhere, this classification is of limited use in understanding negotiated transition in South Africa. Negotiated transition in South Africa essentially is an attempt to end colonial domination in a manner other than colonial withdrawal, as in Algeria, Zimbabwe and Namibia (Slabbert 1992: pp. 13–17), rather than the restructuring of an independent state whose basic identity is not in dispute.

It has been argued that South Africa's latest attempt at transition – while it chronologically forms part of the third of the waves of democratisation that have occurred in the twentieth century – is in fact more akin to 'the nineteenth century democratisations in Europe in which the central feature was the expansion of the suffrage and the establishment of a more inclusive polity' (Dahl, 1991: p. 581). While this view does take cognisance of the major differences between the current mode of transition in South Africa and the Latin American and South European waves, it does, however, underemphasise the 'colonial' dimension that characterises the current South African mode. South Africa – like Zimbabwe – is not a traditional colony, but major and important sections of society do view the transition in quasi-colonial terms. The significance hereof is that an inclination to view certain peoples as non-indigenous – as colonists – translates negatively on a willingness to compromise and share power. Before attempting to assess progress in South Africa's latest attempt at transition, it is necessary to briefly summarise the most important developments in the process of transition since 1990.

The process of negotiated transition to date has generally been portrayed as consisting of a 'talks about talks' phase and a talks-proper phase. This distinction is not used in the brief summary that follows, as it tends to underemphasise the fact that a number of fundamental pre-talk issues – including the issue of violence and the ultimate objective of negotiations – remained unresolved during the second phase. It is far more useful to visualise the transitional process to date as consisting of a first stage lasting until the Inkathagate scandal (July 1991), and a second stage from that date.

De Klerk's opening gambit in February 1990 involved, *inter alia*, the unbanning of the African National Congress (ANC), the Pan-Africanist Congress (PAC) and the South African Communist Party (SACP), the termination of various regulations of the State of Emergency and the release of Nelson Mandela. Following a first round of preliminary talks in London between the ANC and representatives of the South African government at the end of February, a formal meeting between the two parties to identify the major remaining obstacles to negotiations was scheduled for 11 April. This meeting was postponed by the ANC following the death of 11 people in the township of Sebokeng during a protest in March, but the two sides did meet in Cape Town in early May. The government had entered the Cape Town meeting with the intention of bargaining the termination of the ANC's armed struggle in return for agreeing to the lifting of the remaining provisions of the State of Emergency and to the phased freeing of political prisoners. However, there emerged out of the so-called Groote Schuur Minute, only a common commitment towards resolving the existing climate of violence. The working group set up at the meeting was to have reported by the end of May, but differences prevented the tabling of the report until the August summit (the so-called Pretoria Summit) between the government and the ANC. Subsequent to the Cape Town meeting the government did pass a bill providing for indemnity and/or immunity to 'political offenders' (then as yet undefined), and in June lifted the State of Emergency throughout South Africa, except in the violence-racked area of Natal and KwaZulu. In September 1990, following the Pretoria Summit, the phased release of political prisoners began. The ANC suspended the armed struggle, and a joint working-group was appointed to resolve 'outstanding' issues relating to the ANC's suspension of the armed struggle. The ANC's suspension of the armed struggle represented a major departure from the Harare Declaration (Collinge, 1992: p. 4). It indicated that the de Klerk government still held the initiative.

The last quarter of 1990 witnessed little progress in the working-group concerned with the suspension of the armed struggle. There was a temporary halt of the release of political prisoners and the indemnification of exiles, a war of words between the de Klerk government and the ANC, and a threat by Mandela to pull out of negotiations unless the violence was terminated. Within three months of the lifting of the State of Emergency in the Transvaal, unrest areas were declared and emergency powers restored to the armed forces. This was the then low-point of the process of transition. By the end of November no real progress was evident in establishing the working-groups on constitutional issues, a constituent assembly and a new voting system which had been envisaged at the Pretoria Summit.

The initial period of the transitional process relied heavily on the two personalities of de Klerk and Mandela to keep the process afloat. By the end of November 1990 the two leaders had met each other 14 times. In spite of a strong feeling within the ANC at this time that the de Klerk government had not met its promise, Mandela and de Klerk's meeting on 27 November reaffirmed their joint commitment to peaceful solutions and agreed to the establishment of additional joint working-groups to resolve their differences and pave the way for negotiations proper.

The DF Malan Accord of 12 February 1991 was an attempt to resolve ANC–government disagreement as to precisely what the ANC's suspension of armed violence entailed. It was agreed that no political party or movement should have a private army and that Umkhonto we Sizwe (MK) would cease training in South Africa and halt infiltration. There was no agreement on the disclosure of arms caches (Collinge, 1992: p. 11). The ANC itself admitted that it had compromised at DF Malan (*Mayibuye*, March 1991: p. 6). In spite of the provisions of the Accord, disagreement between the government and the ANC as to the release of political prisoners and the return of exiles continued. The Human Rights Commission estimated that approximately 130 political prisoners remained behind bars in early April. The

ANC threatened to suspend all negotiations unless a number of security-related demands (including the dismissal of two security ministers) were met by 9 May 1991. The essential thrust of the government's response was the convening of a multi-party conference on violence at the end of May, which was not attended by the ANC and other organisations on the broad political left, and the announcement of pending legislation for the creation of a standing commission on violence (later to be constituted as the Goldstone Commission). In mid-May the ANC announced the suspension of negotiations until the violence was terminated by the government, but the working-groups on political prisoners/exiles and the suspension of armed activities continued to function. The month of June witnessed the repeal of core apartheid legislation, the Population Registration, Group Areas and Land Acts, but the continued violence and exposure of government funding of the Inkatha Freedom Party (IFP) led to ANC calls for the dismissal of the two ministers, and the establishment of a multi-party commission to monitor and investigate government's alleged role in violence and the secret funding of political parties. De Klerk responded positively on all counts.

Flowing from the May multi-party conference on violence, a National Peace Accord was signed by 29 organisations in mid-September 1991, which included a code of conduct for political parties and for the South African Police. The signing of the Peace Accord led to the resumption of talks between the ANC and government on an all-party conference in mid-October. The Peace Accord involved the creation of the first transitional structures in the process of negotiated transition, and signaled the end of negotiations over preconditions. The three procedural issues which dominated this phase were the release of political prisoners, the indemnification and return of exiles, and the creation of a climate conducive to negotiations – especially as regards violence (Haysom, 1992: p. 35). The Pan-Africanist Congress (PAC) attended the summit which launched the Peace Accord, but refused to sign the Accord. The PAC and AZAPO did, however, decide initially to participate in an all-party conference (subsequently to be named Codesa) after the formation of a Patriotic Front with the ANC in October 1991. The ANC/Cosatu/SACP alliance – the so-called tripartite alliance – exhibited growing confidence in the second half of 1991: a fact highlighted by its identification of the government as the major obstacle to negotiations, the two-day national anti-VAT strike and the growing emphasis on the need for an interim government.

The Convention for a Democratic South Africa, which met formally for the first time in early December 1991, was attended by 19 delegations – the notable absentees being the Conservative Party (CP) and the PAC (which had initially agreed to attend). Seventeen organisations signed a Declaration of Intent, which endorsed the creation of 'an undivided South Africa whose supreme law would be a constitution guarded over by an independent judiciary'. In his speech to the Convention, President de Klerk stated that the government was willing to amend the constitution to 'make an interim power-sharing model possible on a democratic basis'.

Five working-groups were established by the Convention and were given tasks to complete before the second plenary session of Codesa, which was scheduled for March 1992. Their respective briefs were to create a climate conducive to free political participation (including the role of the international community), constitutional principles and a constitution-making body/process, transitional arrangements concerning an interim government, determining the future of the homelands, and establishing time-frames for the implementation of decisions. The working-groups held their first meeting in late January 1992 and, in an attempt to lure the white right into Codesa, de Klerk suggested that the issue of self-determination be formally placed on the agenda. Initial expectations concerning Codesa were high – the ANC going so far as to say that Codesa's work could be completed by April, a transitional government could be operational by September and a new constitution could be adopted by December 1992.

However, differences soon emerged in the various working-groups. Contentious issues included the participation of the Zulu King, the reincorporation of the homelands, the powers of local and regional government, and the precise powers and method of constituting an interim government. Smaller parties also articulated concern that the two major parties – the ANC and NP – were stage-managing the process. Apart from these internal problems, the Codesa process was effectively terminated during the period between de Klerk's announcement of the all-white referendum following the governing party's heavy defeat in a parliamentary by-election and the referendum itself.

Following its overwhelming triumph in the March 1992 referendum, the government adopted a far tougher stance on the ANC's armed struggle, and threatened a postponement of Codesa until the ANC dismantled its armed wing. The government's initial proposals concerning interim executive structures were summarily rejected by the ANC as involving nothing more than advisory powers. However, after initially being opposed to the idea of a transitional government, the de Klerk government grudgingly conceded to the argument that it could not simultaneously be player and referee, and in the second half of 1991 had accepted the need for an interim government. This reflected the increasing influence of the ANC within the process of negotiated transition. At the end of March 1992, the government also accepted the idea of an elected body to write a new constitution within broad principles agreed to at Codesa. A shift in position was also evident in de Klerk's sudden proposal, during his budget vote in parliament, of a rotating two- or three-person presidency during the transitional period. This too was summarily rejected by the ANC. By mid-April the progress in Codesa was so limited that the ANC stated that it would review its participation in the process.

After having been twice postponed, the second plenary session of Codesa was held on 15 May 1992. The ANC and government failed to reach a compromise concerning the majorities required for the adoption of a new constitution and clauses concerning the establishment of regional governments and their powers. The government jettisoned its initial position that a second regionally-based house also be included in the constitution-making process, but demanded a 75 per cent majority for the adoption of regional clauses. The Boipatong incident in mid-June was the straw that broke Codesa's back and the phase of 'substantive' negotiations came to a formal end.

THE ABSENCE OF AN INCLUSIVE MIDDLEGROUND

This second part of the chapter argues that the lack of substantive progress, and the drawn-out nature of the process of negotiated transition in South Africa to date reflect the fact that an inclusive political middleground remains elusive. The middleground is the terrain which South African liberals have traditionally defined as theirs. In this chapter inclusivity is deemed to constitute the core component of this middleground and measured in terms of the effective political participation of all within a given polity (Dahl, 1971: p. 4). An inclusive middle-ground did not exist at the beginning of the process of negotiated transition, because the domestic political scene was characterised by a contest for hegemony between the regime models of 'People's Power' and of 'Technocratic Liberation' (Esterhuyse and du Toit, 1990: p. x). As Slabbert (1992: p. 28) puts it, 'the total strategy of the regime was the National Security Management System and reform, the total strategy of the ANC was the national democratic revolution for a liberated South Africa'. Apart from the contending regime models of the ANC and NP respectively, there were other visions of a 'new' South Africa both on the far left and right, but the ANC's and NP's were unquestionably the dominant models. This is reflected in the progressive polarisation that has occurred within South African politics since February 1990. The non-overlapping nature of the two dominant regime models meant that an essentially zero-sum vision of the conflict was operating. This state of affairs reflected the essential failure of political liberalism in South Africa. This failure was foreshadowed by what has been referred to as the liberal slide-away of the 1980s, and highlighted by the anguished and vitriolic debates in liberal circles at the end of the 1980s as to whether liberal-democratic values would be best served by liberals aligning themselves with one of the two major contending forces. For an analysis of the liberal slideaway, see O'Malley (1989).

The contending regime models of Technocratic Liberation and People's Power that dominated South Africa at the end of the 1980s could be contrasted along three dimensions, namely competing understandings of democracy, and nationhood, and divergent priorities as regards socio-economic public policy (du Toit, 1990: p. 64). Given the fact that modern democracy has no choice but to operate within the nation-state paradigm, the first two of these dimensions are closely related to one another. An outline of the two models will be provided along these three dimensions, showing the models to be mutually exclusive

(Esterhuyse, 1991). First, consideration will be given to the 'national question'.

The NP's Technocratic Liberation model of the late 1980s accepted the idea of one nation composed of distinct racial sub-nations. In Schlemmer's words, 'the concept of the white nation has given way to the concept of the autonomy and lifestyle of white communities within a "multi-racial nation"' (1988: p. 13). By the late 1980s the NP's approach to nation-building (although the party only later started using the term itself) was one of ethnic sub-nationbuilding by a decentralised multi-racial state in which the white sub-nation would enjoy a position of co-determination with the other sub-nations. The approach to nation-building was quasi-Jacobian in the sense that while the state (multi-racial, but white-controlled) led this attempt at 'nation-building' it was aimed at separation, not integration. Giliomee and Schlemmer (1989: p. 166) emphasise that the NP's perspective on the national question remained removed from the liberal ideal of the common society. It envisaged a South African nation as an ethnically heterogeneous one, with whites as a sub-national minority alongside a number of others. The NP thus viewed the South African nation as a nation of ethnic (racially defined) minorities.

The NP's five-year action plan, which was adopted at its 1989 National Congress, reconfirmed the party's commitment to the inclusion of black South Africans in the highest decision-making structures of the state, but the party remained committed to minority or communal autonomy and co-determination for the white sub-nation along with other sub-nations in national concerns (Schlemmer, 1988: p. 26). The idea of nationhood propounded by the ANC People's Power regime model initially promoted the ideal of a single, inclusive, non-racial nation. The model of nation-building was an essentially top-down Jacobian one in which a liberated state would eliminate sub-national or communal loyalties and create a hegemonic, non-racial ethos embodied in a central state. Non-racialism ANC-style is, in fact, the South African version of Nyerere's nation-building dictum, 'Kill the tribe, build the nation'. As articulated by organisations within the Charterist umbrella, non-racialism did not only mean the absence of race-based legislation, but also the refusal to recognise ethnic mobilisation and expression as legitimate. Non-racialism thus demanded the elimination of all forms of political ethnicity (Alexander, 1985: pp. 23–56, 126–53). Private ethnicity would be tolerated to the extent that it did not make claims on the public realm or threaten to make such claims. The ANC's constitutional guidelines in 1988, for example, contained a bill of rights which made provision for the banning of ethnically and/or regionally based political parties or organisations. The promotion of racialism was to be constitutionally proscribed. Non-racial thus not only meant non-ethnic, but also anti-ethnic.

As a result of liberal criticism of these and other parts of the constitutional guidelines (sees Simkins, 1988: pp. 143–5), the ANC began in 1990 to rethink its approach. In spite of the fact that the Freedom Charter recognised the existence of several national groups, the ideal of non-racialism had come to occupy a central plank in Charterist ideology by the late 1980s. Thus the ANC effectively denied that South Africa was a deeply-divided, ethnically heterogeneous society. To the limited extent that racial and ethnic divisions were recognised, they were attributed to apartheid and it was assumed that the demise of apartheid would entail the simultaneous demise of these divisions.

As regards models of democracy, the Technocratic Liberation model of the NP held a purely procedural understanding, in terms of which political power needed to be shared between the racially defined groups in such a manner as to avoid domination of any one racial group by another. Racially defined group rights thus remained official NP party policy at the political level, although the five-year action plan adopted at the party's 1989 Federal Congress did acknowledge that free association across lines of race was essential (Friedman, 1991: p. 177). Since early 1990 the NP's reference to groups and group rights became far less frequent and was replaced by the terms 'minority' and 'minority protection'.

A 1990 pamphlet listed as one of the party's constitutional objectives the absence of 'discrimination on any basis', and referring to democracy stated that 'a simple, simplistic or un-qualified majority government in our heterogeneous country will go hand in hand with instability. A remote single central government will not be sensitive enough to satisfy all the needs of all citizens in all regions' (NP, 1990: pp. 5–6). The NP's regime model had clearly shifted in the direction of a federal state inclusive of the homelands. The establishment of the nine economic development regions during the 1980s which cut across the boundaries of the existing 'independent' homelands and self-governing territories was one of the early signs of changing NP thinking towards a future state structure. But the federal idea was embedded in NP thinking at this time, because the party publication referred to above listed as an additional constitutional objective the establishment of 'a united multi-party democratic state'. This was so in spite of the fact that the party had operated, and been structured since its inception, along federal lines. The reason for the initial hesitancy of the NP in committing itself unequivocally to a federal position is linked to the fact that it had been the constitutional policy of the white liberal opposition parties in South Africa since 1959.

Within the People's Power model, democracy is associated with the notion of distributive justice, and is considered to exist when the substance of public policy provides for an equitable access to opportunities as well as distribution of rewards to all members of society, irrespective of how these public policy decisions are reached (du Toit, 1990: p. 64). To achieve this social democracy, the ANC thus advocated a strong centralised and unitary state unfettered by institutions embodying power-sharing. The central – and potentially hegemonic – role of the state in terms of this model is then countered by the organic links that such a state would have with 'the people' or the working class. Populism remains central to the ANC's model of democracy. Together with the emphasis on distributive and substantive justice, the populist strain constitutes the defining characteristic of the radical democratic vision (Simkins, 1988: pp. 27–30, 109). The question of who are the people – who are to be organically linked to the state, brings one back to the 'national question', and underlies the centrality of this issue in any attempts to resolve the conflict in South Africa.

It is interesting to examine how far these models were diluted by the negotiation process between the two main parties during 1991–92. First we will examine the dimension of the national question. With the scrapping of the Population Registration Act in June 1991, the NP's previous conception of a multi-racial nation based on the four statutorily recognised race-groups officially came to an end. Earlier in the year the NP had proposed a manifesto for the 'New South Africa' which had declared that all people in South Africa should fully participate at all levels of government, but that the rights of all individuals and minorities defined on a non-racial basis needed to be protected in a new constitution. The ANC referred to certain of the clauses in the manifesto as nothing more than a paraphrasing of aspects of ANC policy documents such as the Freedom Charter (*Mayibuye*, March 1991: p. 4). The possibility of the reincorporation of the 'independent' homelands of Transkei, Bophuthatswana, Venda and Ciskei was raised for the first time by de Klerk in March 1991. The NP's later proposal that the nine development regions be used as a starting point in determining suitable regional boundaries for a new dispensation reflected the party's final acceptance of a nation inclusive of all South Africans resident within the boundaries of South Africa prior to the granting of homeland 'independence'. The NP thus committed itself as a signatory of Codesa's Declaration of Intent 'to bring about an undivided South Africa with one nation sharing a common citizenship, patriotism and loyalty'.

The NP's understanding of non-racialism however, differs markedly from that of the ANC. To the former, non-racialism simply means anti-discrimination and is thus shorthand for expressing a commitment to an apartheid-free South Africa. Non-racialism certainly does not mean being anti- or non-ethnic. The party's perspective remains that South Africa is a deeply-divided or ethnically heterogeneous society. Thus, the NP's perspective on the national question changed from a multi-racial perspective based on race classification to a non-racial but ethnic perspective, inclusive of all South Africans (including homeland residents).

With respect to the ANC's position on the national question following the initial period of negotiations, liberal scholars in South Africa have generally tended to emphasise the liberal strain within the ANC (see, for example, Gagiano, 1990: p. 15; Hanf, 1989: p. 108). However, a small number of scholars have made the point that a black or African nationalism remains a strong influence within the ANC (Horowitz, 1991: pp. 13–17; Giliomee and Schlemmer, 1989: pp. 122–5). At the July 1991 National Conference the ANC adopted a Draft Constitution which lists its first aim as being 'to unite all the people of South Africa, Africans in particular, for the complete liberation of the country from all forms of discrimination and national oppression'. Formulations of this kind have a long pedigree in the ANC but what is significant is that the official report of the

Commission on the ANC Constitution minuted that 'there was a view that the words "Africans in particular" in this paragraph be deleted'. The general position arrived at after proper motivation was that the words should not be deleted (ANC, 1991: p. 1). The African nationalist strain within the ANC would appear to have strengthened during the process of negotiation. This is related to the process of Africanisation, whereby coloured and Indian individuals who were prominent in United Democratic Front/Mass Democratic Movement structures have been replaced by black Africans.

The ANC's decision not to amend the wording should also be seen against the background of the fact that the ANC became increasingly sensitive both to its inability to make any real progress in attracting membership among minority groups and to the success that opposition parties experienced in this regard. After opening its membership in the second half of 1990, the NP made substantial progress in attracting coloured support, particularly. It is now estimated – even by scholars sympathetic to the ANC – that up to 70 per cent of the coloured population will vote against the ANC. Tension within the Congress movement around the issue of non-racialism also surfaced in mid-1991 when the ANC and the Transvaal and Natal Indian Congresses decided that the two Indian Congresses would continue to exist as separate entities. A growing sensitivity within the ANC to the ethnic/national question did temporarily emerge in mid-1991. An article on the national question in *Mayibuye* pointedly asked whether 'participation in the ANC is as broad-based and representative as it can and should be' and warned against dismissing the ethnic factor out of hand (June 1991: pp. 24–7). Articles specifically on and aimed at the coloured and Indian communities appeared in editions of *Mayibuye* in the second half of 1991 and early 1992. The ANC implicitly recognised the black African bias of its constituency at its 1991 National Conference and resolved to canvass for greater support in the coloured, Indian and white communities on issues that concerned them.

By mid-1992 the NP's regime model of the most appropriate political structures for a future state had shifted markedly from the power-sharing, state-building perspective that held sway in the late 1980s. Power-sharing remains the lodestar but has now been shorn of its racial (but not ethnic or communal) content. Not only did ethnic or communal (non-racial in the NP's language) power-sharing replace racial power-sharing, but the idea of federalising and constitutionalising the state emerged. A 1990 party pamphlet asserted, 'a simple, simplistic or unqualified majority government in our heterogeneous country will go hand in hand with instability. A remote single central government will not be sensitive enough to satisfy all the needs of all citizens in all regions' (NP, 1990: p. 6). In March 1991 Minister Viljoen for the first time indicated that the government was rethinking its position on regional government and favoured the replacement of the provincial, self-governing and regional services council authorities by autonomous, constitutionally defined political units based on the nine development regions. Without using the term federal, the party proposed regional and local levels of government with 'full legislative and executive functions' which would not be mere 'administrative extensions of the central government' (ibid.). While the principle of a separation of executive, legislative and judicial powers in a future constitution was included in Codesa's Declaration of Intent, the NP's preference for a decentralised state was not. However, unlike the Inkatha and Bophuthatswana delegations, who objected to the clear anti-federalist bias of the declaration, the NP signed the Declaration of Intent.

In contrast to the decentralised, power-sharing perspective of the NP, the ANC's preferred view of a future state remains a strong, centralised entity which can undertake the task of undoing the socio-economic inequalities heightened by apartheid and fully including those excluded from the apartheid state into a new non-racial state. In the period since 1990, the ANC has, however, been far more explicit in its commitment to certain liberal-democratic checks and balances, a Bill of Rights, proportional representation and a multi-party system. Clear tensions, however, exist between these commitments and the populist thrust of the ANC's perspective on democracy. The 1992 policy guidelines do refer to local, regional and national levels of government within a unitary context, but specify that the central parliament 'should determine what powers the regions shall have' (that the scope of regional powers be embodied in ordinary legislation and not in a constitution), that 'regional government should not be able to contradict national policy', and that 're-gional government would have to function broadly within the framework of national policy' (ANC, 1992: pp. 6, 22). The latest

ANC policy-guidelines are, in fact, far more specific on the need for effective and strong *local* government reflecting the strong populist strain. But this does not include regional government. The ANC publicly chastised a Nigerian member of an OAU delegation which had attended Codesa 2, for suggesting the appropriateness of a federal constitution for an ethnically deeply divided society like South Africa. The ANC's views are closely related to its continued perception of itself as a liberation movement representative of the South African people as a whole.

CONSTITUTIONAL REFORM: PROSPECTS FOR THE FUTURE

In spite of an extended period of 'negotiations', the respective regime models of the two major political players remained far removed from one another in mid-1992. The two contending regime models have undergone changes in the period between February 1990 and June 1992, and moved closer towards one another, but on fundamental issues, such as definitions of nationhood, non-racialism, and the structural characteristics of a future state, little progress has been made. The NP's regime model has undergone greater changes than that of the ANC but this is not surprising, given its greater distance from the middle-ground at the inception of negotiated transition, because of its initial adherence to the race-based model. The NP's view on the national question has, in fact, shifted to the position previously solely occupied by the conservative, consociational strain of South African liberalism, hence the progressive marginalisation of a party like the Democratic Party. The NP's current view of the state – as a source of stability which must be written into a future constitution – does not, however, accord with the traditional liberal view of the state.

Changes in the ANC's regime model have been less marked. There has been a toning-down of an initially hostile anti-ethnic perspective, the explicit adoption of certain liberal-democratic mechanisms and a cursory nod in the direction of regionalism (within a unitary state). But the view on the essential nature of South African society (deeply divided or not) remains essentially unchanged and the need for power sharing thus bypassed. Assuming that South Africa (with or without apartheid) will remain an ethnically deeply-divided society, the ANC's People's Power regime model, as currently constituted, would appear to run the risk of not being as inclusive as it perforce needs to be to reassure white and other minority groups. The absence of an overlap on fundamentals between the two major regime models reflects the absence of an inclusive middleground, and underlies the deadlock and subsequent breakdown of negotiations.

In a recent study Donald Horowitz has emphasised the fact that South Africa suffers from 'cognitive dissensus', the absence of agreement as to the basic character of the society, the essence of its major social forces, and the nature of the conflict itself (1991: p. 2). In Horowitz's own words, 'there is the conflict itself, and there is the metaconflict – the conflict over the nature of the conflict'. The contending visions of the two major political players of South Africa reflect the continued existence of this metaconflict – which involves irreconcilable perspectives on whether South Africa is an essentially homogeneous society or an ethnically plural society, and whether capitalism is either the primary or the sole cause of South Africa's economic ills. An attempt was made at Codesa to begin substantive negotiations without there being prior agreement as to what the conflict essentially involved. The joint commitment to Codesa's Declaration of Intent thus superficially hid fundamentally irreconcilable regime visions. A common discourse built around terms like non-racialism and regionalism created the impression of an emerging inclusive middleground and democratisation, but the underlying differences began to force their way to the fore and ultimately precluded any substantive progress. The point has been made that debate as to what democracy is and what type of constitution a society needs 'must be encouraged during the first two phases of transition' (Slabbert, 1992: p. 71). This did not occur in South Africa.

POSTSCRIPT

The breakdown of the process of negotiated transition following the Boipatong incident in mid-1992 was followed by a period of intensified international involvement in the South African problem. The United Nations passed two resolutions in July and August (765 and 772) which respectively authorised a fact-finding mission to South Africa by Cyrus Vance and the deployment of a team of UN observers in South Africa. The Organisation of African Unity, the Commonwealth and the European Community followed suit by shortly thereafter sending their own observers. Growing international involvement – albeit largely of a monitoring and procedural nature – thus characterised the second half of 1992.

Following a series of meetings between Roelf Meyer, Minister of Constitutional Development, and Cyril Ramaphosa, Secretary-General of the ANC, a Record of Understanding was agreed between the South African government and the ANC on 16 September. The parties, *inter alia*, agreed to:

- the need for a democratically elected constituent assembly;
- the creation of an interim or transitional government of national unity;
- the further release of political prisoners to be completed by 15 November; and
- the prohibition of the public display and carrying of all dangerous weapons.

The Inkatha Freedom Party withdrew from the process of transition following the September Record of Understanding, and was instrumental in the formation of the Concerned South African Group or Cosag. Other formations that joined Cosag included the governments of Bophuthatswana and the Ciskei, the Afrikaner Volksunie and the Conservative Party. At the end of October, delegations of the South African government and the Pan-Africanist Congress of Azania met in Gaborone, Botswana. The delegations claimed to have identified certain common ground between the two parties and agreed that 'the political conflict in our country should be resolved through peaceful negotiations'. However, little if any substantive progress was made at the summit in the sense of a convergence in views on a future state.

The next major development in the process of negotiated transition was the South African government's announcement of a timetable for further constitutional reform at the end of November 1992. The timetable, *inter alia*, envisaged the convening of a more inclusive multilateral forum before the end of March 1993, agreement on an interim constitution (including constitutional principles and regional governments), a Transitional Executive Council and Election Commission before the end of May 1993, the enactment of the interim constitution by September 1993 and elections by April 1994.

Politically-related violence remained at unacceptably high levels throughout the second half of 1992 and there was a spate of terrorist attacks – assumed to be by the Azanian People's Liberation Army (APLA) – on white civilians towards the end of the year. The State President publicly called for the strengthening of the National Peace Accord in his opening speech to parliament at the end of January 1993. A planning conference for the new multilateral negotiating forum took place in February and multilateral constitutional negotiations resumed on 1 April. The new forum is more inclusive than Codesa (the PAC, the Afrikaner Volksunie and the Conservative Party are all participating), but it appears unlikely that the new forum will be any more successful than its predecessor. The major players continue to hold widely divergent viewpoints on constitutional policy and the necessity of political power-sharing. The first three months of 1993 have been dominated by the unresolved problem of political violence and disputes concerning symbolic and procedural issues (the centrality of the symbolic political dimension is, of course, simply a reflection of the multi-ethnic nature of the South African polity). Substantive issues have been repeatedly swept under the carpet. After over three years of constitutional negotiations, the parties represented at the reconvened negotiations forum, which began sitting in April 1993, could not even agree on a name for the new forum. A constitutional middleground in South Africa remains as elusive as it ever was.

REFERENCES

African National Congress. 1991. Report of the Commission of the ANC Constitution to the ANC National Conference, July 1991.
African National Congress. 1992. ANC Policy Guidelines for a Democratic South Africa.
Alexander, N. 1985. *Sow the Wind: Contemporary Speeches* (Johannesburg, Skotaville).
Collinge, J. 1992. 'Launched on a Bloody Tide: Negotiating the New South Africa', *South African Review 6* (Johannesburg, Ravan Press).

Dahl, R. 1971. *Polyarchy: Participation and Opposition* (New Haven, Yale University Press).

Dahl, R. 1991. 'How Countries Democratise', *Political Science Quarterly* Vol. 106, no. 4.

du Toit, P. 1990. 'The Contest for the Middleground' in Esterhuyse and du Toit, *The Myth Makers: The Elusive Bargain for South Africa's Future* (Johannesburg, Southern Book Publishers).

Esterhuyse, W. and du Toit, P. (eds). 1990. *The Myth Makers: The Elusive Bargain for South Africa's Future* (Johannesburg, Southern Book Publishers).

Esterhuyse, W. 1991. 'The Normative Dimension of Future South African Political Development', in van Vuuren, Wiehahn, Rhoodie and Wiechers, *South Africa in the Nineties* (Pretoria: HSRC Publishers).

Friedman, S. 1991. 'The National Party and the South African Transition', in Lee, R. and Schlemmer, L., *Transition to Democracy* (Cape Town, Oxford University Press).

Gagiano, J. 1990. 'The Contenders', in Esterhuyse and du Toit, *The Myth Makers: The Elusive Bargain for South Africa's Future*. (Johannesburg, Southern Book Publishers).

Giliomee, H. and Schlemmer, L. (eds). 1989. *Negotiating South Africa's Future* (Johannesburg, Southern Book Publishers).

Hanf, T. 1989. 'The Prospects of Accommodation in Communal Conflicts: A Comparative Study', in Giliomee and Schlemmer, *Negotiating South Africa's Future* (Johannesburg, Southern Book Publishers).

Haysom, N. 1992. 'Negotiating a Political Settlement in South Africa', in Moss, G. and Obery, I. (eds). *South African Review 6.* (Johannesburg, Ravan Press).

Horowitz, D. 1991. *A Democratic South Africa? Constitutional Engineering in a Divided Society* (Cape Town, Oxford University Press).

National Party. 1990. *Action Report*, (Pretoria: Hoofstadpers).

O'Malley, K. 1989. 'The Slideaway in South African Liberalism', Paper read at the Biennial Congress of the Political Science Association of South Africa, Port Alfred, 9–11 October.

Schlemmer, L. 1988. 'South Africa's National Party Government', in Berger, P. L. and Godsell, B. A., *A Future South Africa – Visions and Strategies* (Cape Town, Human and Rosseau).

Simkins, C. 1988. *The Prisoners of Tradition and the Politics of Nationbuilding* (Johannesburg, South African Institute of Race Relations).

Slabbert, F. van Zyl. 1992. *The Quest for Democracy: South Africa in Transition* (Johannesburg, Penguin).

7 The Development of External Mediation

Adrian Guelke

When President de Klerk announced, on 2 February 1990, the unbanning of the African National Congress (ANC), the Pan-Africanist Congress (PAC) and the South African Communist Party (SACP) it seemed that he had removed at a stroke the main justification for external mediation in the South African situation, the need for outside pressure to be brought to bear to facilitate negotiations among the parties to a conflict. It was evident from the outset that his actions by themselves had cleared the way to negotiations. The reaction in the West was that President de Klerk's boldness had done away with the need for further involvement by the international community. The Western powers were keen to reward de Klerk by lifting sanctions as promptly as circumstances would allow. The conditions attached to American sanctions legislation delayed that to 1991 in the case of the United States. The Western powers were also disposed to leave all the negotiations to the South African parties, so as not to complicate the achievement of a deal that reflected the country's balance of political forces. This attitude was buttressed by the absence of a strong legal basis for international involvement in the transition to majority rule in South Africa, as had existed in the cases of the neighbouring states of Namibia and Zimbabwe. The Republic of South Africa was a sovereign, independent state, with a government recognised by the international community. From this perspective, there was little justification for involving the United Nations (UN) in the process. Why then has the role of the UN in the transition grown and why has this development enjoyed the approval of the major Western powers? This chapter will endeavour to answer these questions, after recounting briefly the story of how greater international involvement in the South African transition has come about.

The violence in the townships has provided the main impetus to calls for UN intervention, which have been made periodically since February 1990. Ironically, one of the first calls for the UN to get involved was made by the South African foreign minister, Pik Botha, who suggested in September 1990 that the UN should put pressure on Buthelezi and Mandela to end the strife in the townships. In the light of what is now known about the relationship between the South African government and the Inkatha Freedom Party (IFP), this looks somewhat disingenuous. Of course, Pik Botha was not seeking UN monitoring of the violence, simply public political pressure on the parties concerned. Concerted pressure for external monitors to be sent to South Africa began at the end of March 1992, when a report by a fact-finding mission from the International Commission of Jurists (ICJ) called for international monitoring of the violence. The team of five lawyers spent two weeks in South Africa in March 1992 visiting trouble-spots. They had previously visited South Africa in September 1991, and they drew on both sets of experiences in reaching a judgement about the violence. Their report recommended the creation of a team of approximately a hundred international monitors. The team's task would be to monitor both the law-enforcement agencies and political organisations. The report also recommended that policing in Natal and KwaZulu be brought under unified command. It was particularly critical of the IFP leader, Chief Minister Mangosuthu Buthelezi, whom it described as carrying 'a heavy responsibility for the escalation of the violence' (*Agenda for Peace*, 1992: p. 22).

The report's proposal for external monitors was taken up by groups inside South Africa. When Nelson Mandela visited Alexandra, where there had been an upsurge of violence between residents of the township and hostel-dwellers, early in April, he called for the establishment of an independent international monitoring group as 'the only way we can stop the violence' (*Anti-Apartheid News*, May/June 1992). His demand was supported by an Emergency Summit on Violence which was convened by church leaders on 22 April. Representatives from nineteen organisations, including the ANC, the IFP, the PAC, and the Azanian People's Organisation (AZAPO) attended this summit. It unanimously called for an international mechanism to monitor violence, though the IFP subsequently distanced itself from the decisions of the summit.

INTERNAL PEACE EFFORTS

The background to these calls was the faltering progress of internal efforts to stop the violence. When President de Klerk removed the restrictions on the ANC, the PAC and the SACP, it was against the backdrop of an already high level of political violence, with 1403 fatalities in the course of 1989. The violence was quite naturally an important item in the negotiations between the government and the ANC that followed Nelson Mandela's release. In May the government and the ANC committed themselves to 'the resolution of the existing climate of violence and intimidation from whatever quarter' under the Groote Schuur Minute. In spite of this agreement, the liberalisation of the political process led to an escalation of the level of violence. By the end of June, 1591 people had died in political violence since the start of the year (Cooper *et al.*, 1990: p. xxxvi). There were considerable regional variations in the level of violence. By far the worst-affected region at this point was Natal, where a virtual civil war had existed since 1987 between Inkatha and pro-ANC organisations, as discussed in an earlier chapter. In August 1990 the conflict spread to the Transvaal townships when the IFP launched itself as a nationwide political party. In a two-week period, over 500 people died in political violence. This new peak of violence coincided with the conclusion of a second round of negotiations between the government and the ANC. In terms of the Pretoria Minute, the ANC agreed to an immediate suspension of 'all armed actions' in return for the phased release of various categories of prisoners and the granting of indemnity to others. Early in 1991, the ANC entered into two further agreements designed to end the violence. In January, Mandela met Buthelezi and a joint declaration was issued calling on their followers to end all attacks on the other party immediately. In February, the ANC entered into the DF Malan Accord with the government, which defined more precisely the meaning of 'all armed actions' in the Pretoria Minute.[1]

However, these agreements failed to stem the tide of violence. In five days of fighting between supporters of the ANC and the IFP in Alexandra in March 1991, 50 died. At the beginning of April 1991, the ANC sent an ultimatum to the government, threatening to suspend all negotiations unless the government took a number of steps to deal with the violence. The ANC's demands included the following: the dismissal of Adriaan Vlok as Minister of Law and Order and of General Magnus Malan as Minister of Defence, the dismantling of special counter-insurgency units within the security forces, the appointment of an independent inquiry to probe complaints of misconduct by the security forces, the outlawing of the carrying of 'traditional' weapons, and the phasing-out of hostels. President de Klerk's response was to set up a multi-party conference on violence on 24 and 25 May. Out of the conference, which was boycotted by the ANC, the PAC and AZAPO, came recommendations for a code of conduct to govern the behaviour of political organisations and of the security forces themselves and a programme to restructure the police. At the same time, much emphasis was placed on the need for the improvement of conditions in the townships on the grounds that poverty constituted one of the primary causes of the violence (Cooper *et al.*, 1992: p. 69). The conference also established a 'continuation committee' to carry its work forward. This committee in turn set up a 'facilitating committee' to draw organisations that had not attended the conference into the process. This resulted in a meeting with the ANC, AZAPO and a number of other organisations at the end of June. The outcome was the establishment of yet another committee, a 'preparatory committee'. It included representatives of the government, the ANC and the IFP. Its task was to draw up proposals on the violence to refer back to the parties. The eventual result of this process was the signature of the National Peace Accord on 14 September 1991, by the government, the ANC, the IFP and a number of other organisations.[2]

THE NATIONAL PEACE ACCORD

By the time of the signature of the National Peace Accord, the ANC's hand in negotiations had been strengthened considerably by revelations in July that the government had been covertly funding the IFP. The main provisions of the National Peace Accord included the creation of a standing Commission of Inquiry Regarding the Prevention of Public Violence and Intimidation, the setting up of a National Peace Committee serviced by a National Peace Secretariat and Regional and Local Dispute Resolution Committees, the establishment of a special police unit to investigate allegations of misconduct by the police, and codes of conduct for political parties and the police. Judge Richard Goldstone was appointed chairman of the standing commission in October. In the months before the signing of the accord, there was a sharp increase in the numbers killed in political violence. Violence declined to its previous level by November. According to the South African Institute of Race Relations, in the year as a whole 2672 people died in political violence compared to 3699 in 1990 (Copper *et al.*, 1992: p. xxxiv). The next escalation of violence came in February 1992 after President de Klerk announced that a white referendum on the continuation of the reform process would be held on 17 March.

But if this escalation in the level of violence seemed related to the referendum campaign, the massive affirmation of white support for the reform process brought no respite. In the week after the referendum 72 people died and 210 were injured in political violence, according to the Human Rights Commission in Johannesburg. There were two main sources for the violence: the longstanding conflict in Natal, and the confrontation between residents and hostel-dwellers in Alexandra township in the Transvaal. Both involved conflict between the IFP and the ANC. But the bussing into Alexandra of armed supporters of Inkatha also raised the spectre of the indirect involvement of the security forces, including the South African Defence Force (SADF). *Southscan* claimed that evidence collected by journalists on the *Weekly Mail* indicated 'a probably unbreakable link between Inkatha and the SADF's Directorate of Military Intelligence' (*Southscan*, 3 April 1992). At the same time, the new wave of violence prompted disillusionment with the operation of the National Peace Accord, with the chairperson of Lawyers for Human Rights complaining that it was 'not working at all' (*Southern Africa Report*, 3 April 1992). The chairman of the National Peace Committee, John Hall, an executive director of Barlow Rand, reached a similar conclusion, noting that 'violence is fast becoming a way of life in many areas in South Africa and the structures of the Accord appear to be powerless to stem the tide of unrest' (Hall, 1992).

POLITICAL DEADLOCK AND THE BOIPATONG
MASSACRE

Against this background, the ANC's campaign for international
monitoring began to make headway even before the deadlock at
the second meeting of the Convention for a Democratic South
Africa (Codesa II) and the Boipatong massacre. The Organisation of African Unity (OAU) backed the idea and officially
requested that the issue be debated by the UN Security Council.
It was also supported by the Danish foreign minister, Uffe
Ellemann-Jensen, after his visit to South Africa, and he raised
the issue with other foreign ministers of the European Community (EC). However, at the urging of the British government,
a decision on the question was deferred. The British position
was that it would be wrong to propose international monitoring
in the absence of a request from the South African government
for such assistance, and that remained the British stance until
after the Boipatong massacre. The failure of the South African
government and the ANC to reach agreement at Codesa II on
15 and 16 May, coupled with fresh revelations of governmental
security-force involvement in political violence, added to
international concern over the direction of events in South
Africa. On 10 June, Amnesty International issued a highly critical
report, *South Africa: State of Fear – Security Force Complicity in
Torture and Political Killings, 1990–1992*. But it was the massacre
at Boipatong on 18 June and the shooting of unarmed demonstrators during President de Klerk's ill-judged visit to the
squatter camp that provided the decisive impetus to international action so that even the British government shifted
ground.

What gave the Boipatong massacre such political resonance
was not merely the brutal manner in which 38 people were
killed by IFP-supporting hostel-dwellers, but eye-witness accounts
of the massacre which suggested that there had been security-
force complicity in the killings (*The Independent on Sunday*, 21
June 1992). The timing of the massacre suggested a link with
the ANC's mass action campaign, a link ironically underlined
by attempts by government ministers to put the blame for
violence on the atmosphere created by the mass action campaign
(Davenport, 1992). Following the Boipatong massacre, the ANC

suspended its bilateral negotiations with the government, de-
manding an international inquiry into political violence. A
sharp fall in the value of the financial rand underlined the reaction of foreign investors to the crisis. The government's response was the appointment of foreign experts to assist the
Goldstone Commission. At the same time, there was widespread
speculation in the South African press about international
intervention in the crisis.

On 24 June, the Chairman of the US Senate Foreign Relations
Committee, Paul Simon, was quoted as suggesting that Pretoria
should seek UN help, while the Australian foreign minister,
Senator Gareth Evans, confirmed that there had been soundings
on the sending of a Commonwealth observer mission (*The Star*,
24 June 1992). In an editorial on the same day, *The Star* argued
that 'the Government should take a new and less blinkered look
at some of the proposals for international monitoring that are
emanating from this country's friends abroad'. A week later the
Cape Times declared in an editorial that 'the prospect of international mediation offers hope that the crisis of Boipatong can
be resolved before lasting damage is done to the chances of a
negotiated settlement' (*Cape Times*, 1 July 1992). The next day
The Argus gave banner headlines to a report that President Bush
had sent messages to de Klerk and Mandela, offering American
help 'to rescue SA's peace talks' (*The Argus*, 2 July 1992). In an
editorial welcoming this development, entitled 'Baker the
Broker?', *The Argus* argued that 'some form of international
brokering may be the only way to get the negotiating process
going again' (*The Argus*, 3 July 1992).

MONITORING AND ENDING THE NEGOTIATIONS IMPASSE

While the issue of violence had provided the initial impetus for
calls for international involvement, it had become intertwined
with the breakdown of the negotiating process. Thus, the
Johannesburg *Sunday Times* reported 'Western diplomats' as
being of the view that '[de Klerk's] failure to address the ANC's
demands on violence would make it difficult for negotiators
within the ANC to convince their constituency to return to talks'

(*Sunday Times*, 5 July 1992). All this activity culminated in a meeting of the UN Security Council on the issue. The Security Council debated the situation in South Africa on 15 and 16 July. Not merely did the South African Minister of Foreign Affairs, Pik Botha, and Nelson Mandela speak in the debate, the Security Council also heard contributions from Chief Buthelezi, Ken Andrew, on behalf of the Democratic Party, two homeland leaders, and a representative of the Indian House of Delegates. Unusually for deliberations of the UN on the subject of South Africa, the debate received extensive television and press coverage inside South Africa. At the end of the debate, the Security Council unanimously adopted Resolution 765 which, *inter alia*, expressed concern at the breakdown of negotiations, condemned the escalation of violence in South Africa, making particular reference to events in Boipatong, called for effective implementation of the National Peace Accord, and underlined the importance of all parties cooperating in the resumption of the negotiations process. In effect, the resolution balanced criticism of the failure of the South African authorities to deal effectively with violence and implicit pressure on the ANC to go back to the negotiating table. But the most important element of the resolution was the invitation to the UN Secretary-General 'to appoint, as a matter of urgency, a Special Represent-ative of the Secretary-General in order to recommend ... measures which would assist in bringing an effective end to the violence and in creating conditions for negotiations leading towards a peaceful transition to a democratic, non-racial and united South Africa...'.[3]

Following the passage of the resolution, the Secretary-General appointed Cyrus Vance as his special representative. Assisted by a small team from the Secretariat, Vance visited South Africa between 21 and 31 July. In the course of his visit he held discussions with a very wide range of political parties and interest groups. With a few exceptions, such as the Conserva-tive Party, which rejected any foreign involvement in the situ-ation as a contravention of Article 2, paragraph 7 of the UN Charter, Vance found general support for UN monitoring of the violence. But his mission did encounter considerable scepticism from political commentators in South Africa. For example, Ken Owen argued that the main problem was the diminished political authority of de Klerk and Mandela and their inability to control their followers after the failure of Codesa II. He saw the range and variety of interventions by other lesser players, among whom he included Vance and the UN, as simply a vivid demonstration of the weakness of de Klerk and Mandela. Owen gloomily concluded that the country had been delivered into the 'capricious hands ... of the anarchists of street theatre, and the militarists who watch the rising disorder with lip-smacking anticipation' (Owen, 1992). Fuel for such fears of civil conflict was provided by the looming confrontation between the government and the ANC over the next phase of the ANC's rolling campaign of mass action.

Vance also encountered widespread concern that the general strike the ANC had called for 3 and 4 August might lead to violence. As the Secretary-General, Boutros Boutros-Ghali, noted in his report of 7 August to the Security Council:

> [I]t was necessary, even during the mission, to ensure that the mass actions scheduled for 3 August did not erupt into uncontrollable violence despite the wishes of all parties concerned.... It was therefore necessary for my Special Representative and me to take certain exceptional interim measures aimed at preventing, if possible, such a catastrophic possibility. (Boutros-Ghali, 7 August 1992, paras 58–9)

The Secretary-General wrote to de Klerk, Mandela, and Buthelezi to express the UN's anxieties. Mandela suggested that the UN send observers to witness the ANC's demonstrations. After Vance discussed the matter with de Klerk, the South African President indicated that he had no objection to the despatch of UN observers to South Africa for this purpose. As a result a team of ten UN observers monitored the campaign of mass action as it reached a climax during the week beginning 3 August.

In the course of the week, 48 people died in political violence, but there was no general breakdown of order and the major demonstrations of the week passed off relatively peacefully. Thus, the political correspondent of *The Argus*, Frans Esterhuyse, concluded that the outcome of the week's mass action campaign was a 'triumph for the peace-makers' and among 'the heroes who saved the day' he included 'United

Nations observers whose presence clearly encouraged restraint' (*The Argus*, 8 August 1992). It was a common view. In two episodes, in particular, the UN observers were credited with averting bloodshed: a confrontation between ANC marchers and the Ciskei's security forces on the road to the homeland's capital, Bisho, and a showdown between ANC demonstrators and supporters of the extreme right wing, Afrikaner Weerstandsbeweging, in Krugersdorp. The perceived success of UN monitoring was reflected in the reaction to reports that Vance had proposed a continued and increased UN presence. In an editorial entitled 'The Vance Plan is an Advance', *The Argus* concluded: 'Given the manifestly positive role played by 10 UN observers during the week of mass action, further help can hardly be unwelcome, especially since it is abundantly clear that past efforts by the government have failed' (*The Argus*, 8 August 1992). The success of the UN observers during the week of mass action rubbed off on the Vance mission as a whole, leading to suggestions that he might make the ideal mediator in negotiations on the constitution between the government and the ANC. In the event, it was the UN Secretary-General, Boutros Boutros-Ghali, who recommended in his report to the Security Council that the UN should 'make available some 30 observers to serve in South Africa, in close association with the National Peace Secretariat, in order to further the purposes of the Accord' (Boutros-Ghali, 1992, para. 76). He suggested that, as necessary, their number could be supplemented by the addition of observers from other appropriate international organisations such as the Commonwealth, the EC and the OAU. On 17 August, the Security Council unanimously approved the despatch of the extra UN observers as a matter of urgency, while leaving the precise number to be determined by the Secretary-General (*The Star Weekly*, 19 August 1992).

The arrival of UN monitors did not end the violence. Their presence along with monitors from a number of other organisations failed to prevent further massacres, most notably a massacre of 29 ANC supporters by members of the Ciskei Defence Force in Bisho on 7 September 1992. However, the reporting of the monitors did affect the interpretation of the violence and their criticism of the conduct of the security forces put further pressure on the government in its negotiations with even when their actions severely embarrassed the government, such as the extraordinary plot to murder a South African police defector in London in April, which *The Independent* (15 July 1992) revealed on the first day of the Security Council debate on South Africa. According to *The Independent*, the plot involved three members of a Loyalist paramilitary organisation from Northern Ireland and two South African agents, including, amazingly, the personal assistant of the Chief of South African Military Intelligence. On the face of it, it was clear evidence that parts of the South African security apparatus were out of control, as Chapter 4 in this volume explains.

Only after the Goldstone Commission acquired definitive documentary evidence implicating sections of the security forces in a continuing campaign of dirty tricks to undermine the ANC and a further internal inquiry into the allegations, did de Klerk act to purge the security forces. On 19 December 1992, at a hastily-arranged press conference, President de Klerk announced the dismissal or suspension of 23 Defence Force officers, including two generals. In doing so he effectively confirmed that there was a 'third force' within the security forces intent on preventing the ANC's accession to power, a proposition which he had hitherto always denied. But even after this purge, a number of high-ranking officers who have frequently been named in connection with dirty tricks operations against the ANC remain at their posts. Nevertheless, the action against 23 officers in itself is likely to act as a deterrent against a continuation of dirty tricks operations from within the security forces, as is de Klerk's unequivocal condemnation of such activity.

The political effect of de Klerk's action, notwithstanding the ANC's faint praise, has been to reinforce the new relationship between the National Party and the ANC, underlined by a three-day conclave in the first week of December between leading figures in the National Party and the ANC. International monitors did not play a direct role in the sequence of events that led to the purge. That Military Intelligence was continuing to employ the services of a former member of the notorious Civil Cooperation Bureau in activities to subvert the ANC came to light in a court case. That prompted action by investigators for the Goldstone Commission who seized documents from a the ANC. The ANC's hand had also been strengthened by the success of its two-day general strike and of its mass demonstrations, including the march on Pretoria, in August 1992. The ANC's capacity to mobilise the urban African population so effectively in the face of concerted opposition by the government proved the organisation's indispensability and this was reflected in a softening of the government's anti-ANC rhetoric. That paved the way to informal talks between the government and the ANC over the ANC's preconditions for the resumption of negotiations.

On 26 September 1992, President de Klerk and Nelson Mandela signed a Record of Understanding, ending the suspension of formal negotiations between the two sides. It contained four key points of agreement on broad parameters of how a new constitution should be drafted, on the release of prisoners convicted of politically-motivated offences before October 1990, on the fencing of hostels, and on the prohibition of the carrying of dangerous weapons in public places. Chief Buthelezi reacted angrily to the Record of Understanding, which he saw as a threat to Inkatha's place in a broad anti-ANC alliance with the National Party. There was also criticism within the National Party of de Klerk's concessions to the ANC, reflecting divisions within the party over the issue of a deal with the ANC. The hand of those favouring a deal was strengthened by a concession by the ANC: its acceptance in a discussion document made public in November of the need for joint rule with the National Party for a period of up to ten years after the end of the holding of democratic elections. At the same time, further revelations of misconduct by the security forces were undermining the feasibility of alternative strategies based on the construction of an anti-ANC majority. In this context, international monitoring of political violence constituted an important deterrent against any countenancing of, or collusion in, the use of violence to limit the ANC's political influence.

PRETORIA'S ACCEPTANCE OF UN MONITORING

From the UN's perspective, its involvement in the transition in South Africa follows quite naturally from its previous engagement with the issue. The reference in Resolution 765 to four previous resolutions of the Security Council dating back to 1976 underlined that interest, as did previous reports of the Secretary-General on the subject for the General Assembly, including a lengthy report on the progress of negotiations, issued in September 1991 (*Progress Report*, September 1991). The real change has been in the attitude of the South African government towards UN involvement. Why Pretoria has reversed its previous opposition to a UN role in the transition is open to a number of interpretations. The simplest is that de Klerk was forced to give ground by the strength of international reaction to the massacre at Boipatong and the consequent 'prospect of a return to isolation' (*Southern African Report*, 3 April 1992). Another is that a change in attitude towards monitoring by key foreign allies of the government, particularly Britain, was responsible for the shift in the South African position (*Southscan*, 26 June 1992). A third view is that the change is a product of the government's realisation that in the prevailing conservative international political climate, internationalisation may actually assist the government to achieve its objectives (*Southern Africa Report*, 3 July 1992). These interpretations are not necessarily mutually exclusive. A combination is possible, though the first tends to suggest that the government's acceptance of international monitoring stemmed from a position of weakness and the third tends to suggest government confidence in the strength of its position.

The difficulty of interpreting the government's response to international pressures is linked to the problem of explaining the government's stance on the whole issue of violence. Prior to the white referendum on 17 March 1992, President de Klerk's failure to reform the security forces could be attributed to political weakness and to the need to sustain white majority support for the reform process. Following his triumph in the referendum, it became harder and harder to provide an innocent explanation for his reluctance to get rid of elements in the security apparatus that continued to treat the ANC as an enemy of the state. Some liberal commentators, such as Sparks, concluded that weakening and destabilising the ANC through violence was deliberate government policy (Sparks, 1992). However, little appeared to be done to rein in the security forces

Military Intelligence operations centre. Their report led de Klerk to appoint Lieutenant-General Steyn to carry out an inquiry into the activities of Military Intelligence and to report back to the President personally. That might all have happened without international monitoring. However, the presence of external monitors does make it more difficult for evidence of misconduct by members of the security forces that comes to light to be ignored by agencies wishing to retain their international credibility.

While the role played by elements in the security forces in promoting township violence has long featured in international press reports of the conflict in South Africa, even in the second half of 1992, commentators in South Africa, such as Lawrence Schlemmer, were throwing doubt on both the existence and the significance of 'Third Force' involvement in the violence (Schlemmer, 1992, pp. 60–4). Further, analysis in the South African media of the violence has tended to spread the blame for the killings among South Africa's political factions generally. If the government's commitment to constitutional methods was questioned, then so too was the ANC's, particularly in relation to its refusal to disband its armed wing, Umkhonto we Sizwe, and other steps the ANC had taken so as to maintain the option of resuming the 'armed struggle'. Violent activities of township self-defence units, including necklacing and extortion, prompted some strong criticism of the ANC, while at the end of 1992, the actions of the Azanian People's Liberation Army, an organisation linked to the PAC, became the focus of attention as a result of attacks on white civilians. The larger threat that security-force involvement in the violence poses to the establishment of a liberal-democratic dispensation in South Africa has generally received more emphasis internationally than in South Africa.

MONITORING AND MEDIATION

It might be argued that the South African government's acceptance of monitoring falls short of an acceptance of UN mediation. However, most writers on mediation include monitoring as a low-level form of mediation. For example, Oran Young characterises the objectives of mediation as 'informational (offering information, increasing communication), tactical (offering services and resources), conceptual (offering ideas for settlement), and supervisory (monitoring agreements)' (Hoffman, 1992, p. 266). The action of the Security Council in authorising the monitoring of the violence clearly falls under the last of these. Thus, in terms of this characterisation, the dispatch of UN observers to assist in the implementation of the National Peace Accord can in itself be regarded as a form of external mediation. Admittedly, mediation is usually simply thought of as the process of promoting agreement between parties in conflict. But there are a variety of ways in which they may be assisted to this end and monitoring of various kinds is commonly one of them, justifying its inclusion within the general framework of mediation.

However, in any event, UN involvement in the transition has already gone beyond just providing monitors. The deeper UN commitment, reflected in the pressure the UN Secretary-General has put on the government to implement a long list of recommendations for curbing the violence and in the pressure put on the ANC to return to the negotiating table, is a measure of what is at stake for the organisation in South Africa. As a result of the decisions of the Security Council, the prestige of the United Nations is now bound up with the success of the National Peace Accord, notwithstanding the fact that the UN observers operate independently of the local structures created to implement it. Further, it is well understood by the UN that the fate of the Accord depends at least as much on the political climate as it does on the capacity of small numbers of international monitors to deter political violence by exposing the miscreants. In this context, the fervour of the Secretary-General's advocacy of the resumption of negotiations shows his awareness of the strain that the absence of an agreement on the country's constitutional future places on the National Peace Accord and consequently on the success of UN intervention (Boutros-Ghali, 1992, para. 79).

PROSPECTS FOR INTERNATIONAL MEDIATION IN SOUTH AFRICA

In their account of international mediation, Zartmann and Touval describe mediation as 'an intervention acceptable to the adversaries in the conflict who cooperate diplomatically with the intervenor' (Zartmann and Touval, 1985: p. 31). They argue that while the aim of conflict resolution or abatement gives legitimacy to this form of third-party intervention, the motives for mediation are unlikely to be found simply in altruism. The same applies to the parties themselves. Their acceptance of mediation is also likely to be rooted in perceptions of whether mediation will advance their interests rather than a simple desire for peace. They argue that the parties' acceptance of a mediator does not depend on whether they perceive the mediator to be impartial but, at the same time, 'mediators must be perceived as having an interest in achieving an outcome acceptable to both sides' (Zartmann and Touval, 1985, p. 37). They describe three roles that mediators can play. The role of communicator, of acting as a telephone-line between the parties, is the least important and most passive. The next level is that of formulator, in which the mediator does more than serve as a messenger between the parties by initiating proposals. Finally, the mediator as manipulator utilises powers to shift the positions of the parties so as to make agreement possible.

They contend that the headway made by mediation in large part depends on the leverage the mediator has over the parties. According to Zartmann and Touval,

> Leverage comes, first, from the parties' need for a solution that the mediator can provide; second, from the parties' susceptibility to shifting weight that the mediator can apply; and third, from the parties' interest in side payments that the mediator can either offer ('carrots') or withhold ('sticks'). (Zartmann and Touval, 1985, p. 40)

By applying this model of international mediation to the UN's intervention in South Africa, strengths and weaknesses of external mediation in the South African transition can be identified. No foreign power would seem to have vital interests at stake in the outcome of the transition in South Africa nor, for that matter, do the stakes for the international community as a collective entity seem particularly high. Conflict in South Africa has little strategic importance compared to the potentiality for wider conflict in the Middle East, in the Balkans, or among the republics of the former Soviet Union, especially against the backdrop of the existence of a superpower's nuclear arsenal in their midst. Indeed, in this light, the fact that external mediation has taken place in South Africa even on a limited basis might be considered surprising. One possible explanation is that there remains an underlying sensitivity among major powers to the potentially destabilising impact of a racial conflagration in South Africa on Western society. In particular, Britain would want to avert any situation that led to a large exodus of whites from South Africa, because of the large number of British passport-holders among them.

Another possible explanation is that the UN's involvement is primarily a legacy of its previous engagement with the issue, reflecting the importance of Third World concerns within the organisation during the Cold War. A third possible explanation is that external mediation in the case of South Africa and a number of other conflicts is, on the contrary, a consequence of the recent changes in the international political system. In particular, it can be argued that the ending of bipolarity, as a result of the collapse of the Soviet Union, has removed at a stroke a whole series of constraints on external intervention, including mediation. Changes in international norms, particularly the lifting of the longstanding anathema against secession and the increasing assumption of the existence of a right of intervention in cases of oppression of minorities, highlighted by the establishment of a safe haven for the Kurds in Iraq, have also provided an impetus towards the internationalisation of ethnic conflicts. The dangers of international involvement are well illustrated by what has happened to Yugoslavia. Disillusionment with the consequences of such efforts may lead to the establishment of new constraints, though at this point it is difficult to see how such constraints could be justified in the light of the present interpretation of international norms. The first and third seem to me the most persuasive explanations, with most weight on the third. If one assumes that the stakes for the rest of the world in the outcome of the transition in South Africa are relatively small, then this must be considered a weakness, limiting the extent to which extra resources will be committed to the situation if things go wrong, notwithstanding the loss of prestige the UN would suffer as a result of failure.

However, the leverage available to the UN can be seen as a strength of its external mediation. Both the National Party and the ANC are widely perceived as being desperate to achieve a negotiated settlement that enjoys international legitimacy

(Laurence, 1992). The former because of the economic consequences of a continuing impasse; the latter because of the high
cost of achieving its objectives through any other route. Indeed,
the fact that they came close to an agreement at Codesa II is
evidence of their desperation rather than of the compatibility of
their goals. While international legitimacy might be conferred
on a wholly internal settlement between the National Party and
the ANC, the UN's involvement would guarantee it. The perception of a settlement lacking international legitimacy would be
that it had not fully resolved the conflict. The settlement that
made Bishop Abel Muzorewa the Prime Minister of a country
called Zimbabwe-Rhodesia is the obvious precedent in this
respect.

In respect of the second source of leverage that Zartmann
and Touval put forward, the domination of the UN Security
Council by the Western powers places the Secretary-General in
a strong position to lean on both sides. In respect of the third
source, the Secretary-General may even be in a position to help
bring about the trade-off that offers the best hope of overcoming South Africa's political impasse: economic assurances for
the whites in return for their acceptance of qualified majority
rule. Although the South African government would prefer to
limit the scope of international involvement in the transition so
that it did not extend much beyond its own foreign appointees
to the Goldstone Commission, the UN observers it has already
accepted, and the inevitable monitoring (official or otherwise)
of the country's first one-person-one-vote elections, the scenario
sketched above of deeper external involvement in the negotiating process no longer seems far-fetched. The deaths of over
7000 people in political violence since Mandela's release provide ample evidence of the fragility of the situation in South
Africa. It may reasonably be interpreted as an indication that
the country needs external help in making the transition from
white minority rule to a new dispensation.

CONCLUSION

In a chapter on mediation in the post-Cold War world, Mark
Hoffman refers to 'over-reliance on particular forms of conflict
management – be they coercive diplomacy, leveraged media-

tion, or facilitative problem-solving' (Hoffman, 1992: p. 280). He argues that with a better understanding of the possibilities of mediation, it will be possible to approach protracted conflicts, among examples of which he includes South Africa, 'with the ability to deploy a complex and varied range of complementary third-party initiatives in support of sustainable integrative solutions' (Hoffman, 1992: p. 280). The dispatch of UN observers to monitor political violence represents just one aspect of international engagement in events in South Africa. The extent to which the negotiating stances of the parties have been shaped by all manner of external influences is worth underlining. A small indication of that is the fact that Mandela and de Klerk have spent as much time and effort in wooing international opinion over the last two years as they have their own constituencies in South Africa. In this respect, the distinction between an externally mediated and an internal settlement can be overdrawn. As the presence of UN, EC and OAU observers at Codesa II emphasised, any agreement on the future of South Africa is likely to be the product of some degree of external involvement, at least indirectly, and to be subject to a very wide measure of international scrutiny.

Further, too much should not be taken for granted in a negotiating process that has already seen many ups and downs. The cordial relations established between the leaders of the National Party and the ANC at the end of 1992 may prove difficult to sustain, as the distance between their political objectives becomes apparent during the bargaining on a new constitution. In that case, UN mediation can be expected to try to bridge the gap. In this context, the extent to which violence has eroded trust between blacks and whites should not be underestimated. This has tended to be obscured by the emphasis that has been placed on rivalry between the ANC and Inkatha and even more by the characterisation of that conflict in simplistic ethnic terms. Although antipathy between Zulu and Xhosa migrant workers has played a slight part in some of the violence in the Transvaal townships, it is a minor element even there. It is worth underlining that much of the killing has been in Natal among Zulus and also that Inkatha enjoys very little popular support in comparison with the ANC, as an earlier chapter points out. In the long run the PAC may prove a more durable threat to accommodation between white and black in South Africa than the government's doomed attempts to construct a conservative political majority among blacks through bolstering figures such as Chief Buthelezi.

The absence of traditions of political tolerance, the long history of the oppressive use of the power of the state, and the use of government patronage to reward friends and punish enemies constitute obvious obstacles to the establishment and survival of liberal-democratic norms in South Africa. External mediation may be needed to ensure that every adult is able to participate in the creation of a new political order. Government policy, particularly in the economic field, is also likely to be influenced by external opinion, particularly given the leverage available to the international community over decisions on the economy, and that influence may be sustained into the future. However, beyond the transition from white minority rule, one can predict that external influences on the conduct of politics in South Africa will decline. In the long run, therefore, the capacity of the country to transcend its unhappy political past is likely to depend on South Africans themselves, however important the role played by external mediation in the actual transition to a new dispensation turns out to be.

NOTES

1. The text of the Groote Schuur Minute, the Pretoria Minute, the agreement between the ANC and the IFP in January 1992, and the DF Malan Accord are included in full as appendices in Cooper *et al.*, 1992: pp. 512–21.
2. The text of the National Peace Accord is included in full as an appendix in Cooper *et al.*, 1992: pp. 522–58.
3. The text of Resolution 765 is quoted in full at the head of the Secretary-General's report on South Africa, Boutros-Ghali, 7 August 1992, para. 1.

BIBLIOGRAPHY

Agenda for Peace: An Independent Survey of the Violence in South Africa by the International Commission of Jurists (Geneva, International Commission of Jurists, June, 1992).

Anti-Apartheid News, May/June 1992 (London).
The Argus, 2 July 1992 (Cape Town).
The Argus, 3 July 1992 (Cape Town).
The Argus, 8 August 1992 (Cape Town).
Boutros-Ghali, Boutros. 7 August 1992. *Report of the Secretary-General on the Question of South Africa* (New York, United Nations, S/24389).
Cape Times, 1 July 1992 (Cape Town).
Cooper, Carole *et al.* 1990. *Race Relations Survey 1989/90* (Johannesburg, South African Institute of Race Relations).
Cooper, Carole *et al.* 1992. *Race Relations Survey 1991/92* (Johannesburg, South African Institute of Race Relations).
Davenport, Rodney, 29 June 1992, 'Sinister Links Seen at Root of Current Crisis', *Cape Times* (Cape Town).
Hall, John, May 1992, 'The Peace Accord – quo vadis?', *South Africa Foundation Review* (Johannesburg).
Hoffman, Mark. 1992. 'Third-Party Mediation and Conflict-Resolution in the Post-Cold War World' in John Baylis and N. J. Rengger, *Dilemmas of World Politics* (Oxford, Clarendon Press).
The Independent, 15 July 1992 (London).
The Independent on Sunday, 21 June 1992 (London).
Laurence, Patrick, June 1992, 'The Issue of Political Power Behind the Deadlock at Codesa II', *South Africa Foundation Review* (Johannesburg).
Owen, Ken, 26 July 1992, 'Kings Rule, or Barons, or the Upstarts Take Over', *Sunday Times* (Johannesburg).
Progress Report on the Implementation of the Declaration of Apartheid and its Destructive Consequences in Southern Africa: Second Report of the Secretary-General, 4 September 1991 (New York, United Nations, A/45/1052).
Reynolds, N. 1990. 'Planning for Education Expansion in Zimbabwe', in B. Nasson and J. Samuel (eds), *Education: From Poverty to Liberty* (Cape Town, David Philip).
Schlemmer, Lawrence, October 1992, 'Violence – What Is To Be Done?', *South Africa International* 23: 60–4.
South Africa: State of Fear – Security Force Complicity in Torture and Political Killings, 1990–1992, June 1992 (London, Amnesty International).
Southern Africa Report, 3 April 1992 (Johannesburg).
Southern Africa Report, 3 July 1992 (Johannesburg).
Southscan: A Bulletin of Southern African Affairs, 26 June 1992 (London).
Southscan: A Bulletin of Southern African Affairs, 3 April 1992 (London).
Sparks, Allister, 2 July 1992, 'ANC Forced into a Corner as de Klerk Plays for Time', *Cape Times* (Cape Town).
The Star, 24 June 1992 (Johannesburg).
The Star Weekly, 19 August 1992 (Johannesburg).
Sunday Times, 5 July 1992 (Johannesburg).
Zartmann, I. William and Touval, Saadia, Summer 1985, 'International Mediation: Conflict Resolution and Power Politics', *Journal of Social Issues* 41: 27–45.

Index